LEARN
to surf ™
LOCALITY GUIDES
Bondi

LEARN to surf™

LOCALITY GUIDES

Bondi

m Messenger Publishing

messenger

© Messenger Publishing
First published 2008 by Messenger Publishing
PO Box H241, Australia Square, NSW 1215
www.messengerpublishing.com.au

Distributed in Australia by Gary Allen
For further information about orders:
Phone: +61 2 9725 2933
Email: customerservice@garyallen.com.au

Cover image: Claire Norman at Bondi Beach, courtesy of Lets Go Surfing Bondi

Internal imagery: Please see photography credits at the rear of this book. The publisher has made every effort to properly credit every photographer and individual used in this book. If you feel a photograph has been used incorrectly, please contact the publisher so it can be rectified for the next print run.

Design: Heidi Helyard
Editing: Anna Crago
Printed in China through Messenger Print Brokerage
Legal counsel: HWL Ebsworth Lawyers

Learn to Surf Locality Guide: Bondi
Messenger Publishing
ISBN 978-0-9805112-0-8 (paperback)
10 9 8 7 6 5 4 3 2
Cataloguing-in-Publication Data is available from the National Library of Australia

www.learntosurfguides.com.au

DEDICATION

To David Price – thanks for taking me for my first surf
(and practically killing me on my second) and for constantly
believing in me.

Lisa x

Foreword

Barton Lynch

I can still remember my first surf some 38 years ago, a day that changed my life forever. It was at kiddies' corner at Palm Beach in NSW. I remember hating the first half hour or so as the conditions weren't quite right for a beginner. The tide was too high, the waves were hard to catch, and they were dumping onto the shore. I remember coming in and saying to my dad that I didn't want to do it anymore, but he convinced me to wait a little while and give it another go. By the time I ventured back out to sea, the tide had dropped enough to allow the waves to break and make them easier to catch. They were rolling evenly towards the shore and I managed to stand up on my first wave all the way to the beach. I rode wave after wave for the next hour and for that matter have continued to ride them to this day.

There is something particularly special about gliding on a piece of energy that has been produced by the natural way of the world. Even though the wave has finally reached the end of its life, it still provides you with so much joy before it disappears, never to be seen again. That wave can never be reproduced and if you are not there in that moment you will never know that it even existed.

This is why you can't just surf as a hobby – it's all-consuming and addictive. Once the surfing bug has bitten, you will never be the same person again. The things you thought were important before do not have the same value anymore. You will spend your time hunting and dreaming of the perfect wave and you will be liberated from the shackles of an ordinary life by the integrity of the pursuit.

When you paddle off terra firma into the great big blue you will leave all your worries and problems behind – because you cannot survive out there unless you are living in the moment and giving total concentration to the fun at hand.

Us Aussies are in love with the beach and the lifestyle that it gives. There is not much else that we really want to do with our lives besides get to the coast, swim in the ocean, ride a few waves, throw in a fishing line and catch some lunch, check out the beautiful surroundings and people and then share a beer to reflect on the great time had.

Whether you're a grommie or a grey brigade first timer, do not listen to those who say you can't do it, and do not take no for an answer. Never give up because surfing – like all things worth doing – takes time, commitment and focus to get to the point where the rewards outweigh the effort.

There are inherent rewards in just being in the ocean, but when you get to the stage where you can ride the tube, you will know why most people say that it is better than sex.

If I can you give you a few quick bits of advice they would be: 1) make sure that you are a strong swimmer before you try to surf because if you can swim, you can save your life and greatly reduce the risks; 2) be happy to go slowly and learn with baby steps; 3) respect Mother Nature and acknowledge that she is always the boss; and 4) understand that the best surfer is the one with the biggest smile.

Get out there, share in the dream and make yours come true.

BL (Barton Lynch, 1988 World Champ)

X

Foreword – Barton Lynch   viii
Introduction – Lisa Messenger   xvi

WELCOME TO BONDI   1

Snapshot   4
History   6
Interesting facts   6
Surfing at Bondi   8
Bondi from the air   10
Rules of the beach   16
Profile – Rod Kerr,
Bondi Lifeguard   18
Nearby breaks   22
Tips for Bondi learners   24

Profile – Brenda Miley   26
Profile – Big Wave Dave   30

1. So you want to surf   32
Can't start without   34
Short history of surfing   36
Profile – Layne Beachley   46
Styles of surfing   50
Understanding the ocean   56
How waves are created   58
Profile – Tom Carroll   60
Offshore and onshore   68
Rips   70
Profile – Pam Burridge   72

Contents

Sweeps	80
Tides and their impact	81
Understanding the weather	82
Profile – Dayyan Neve	84
Fit to surf?	88
2. Getting organised	**96**
The beginners toolkit	98
Types of surfboard	100
Aussies and the surfboard	102
Anatomy of a surfboard	104
Tail options	106
Profile – Ben Macartney, Coastalwatch	108
Where do I fit?	110
Which board for me?	112
Hard or soft boards	114
Waxing boards	116
Maintaining your board	118
Profile – Danny Wills	120
What to wear	124
Do I need lessons?	134
Profile – Barton Lynch	136
3. Surf theory	**140**
Paddling	142
Goofy or natural?	144
Tackling the white water	148

Hanging out on your board 158

Turning your board around 160

Profile – Stephanie Gilmore 162

A bit about waves 164

Types of wave breaks 166

Parts of a wave 168

Waves for beginners 170

Catching your first wave 172

Profile – Rusty Miller 174

Standing up 178

Catching green waves 182

Profile – Eugene Tan 186

The lineup 192

Turns and cool stuff 194

Wipeouts 204

Profile – Midget Farrelly 208

4. Surf rules and safety 210

Surf etiquette 213

Profile – Martin Grose 216

Surf safe tips 220

Nasties to look out for 224

Profile – Perth Standlick 230

Your medical kit 232

Basic first aid for surfers 234

5. Road trips and hot spots 236

Road trip tips 241

Profile – Derek Recio,
Tracks Magazine   244
Hot surf spots in Australia   246

6. Resources   252

People you need to know   254
Surf lingo   258

HANGING AT BONDI   260

Welcome to Waverley   262
Getting there   263
Places to eat and drink   264
Shopping   275
Services   278

Alcohol-free zones   281
Places to stay   282
Things to do   284
Local markets   288
Annual events   288
Beyond Bondi   289
Useful websites   293
Profile – Gyton Grantley   294
Profile – Mojada   296

Acknowledgements   300
Sponsor's gallery   304
Messenger Publishing   308
Photo credits   310

Introduction
Lisa Messenger

I'm a bit of an adrenalin junkie and have always had a love affair with all things beachy. So when I went out for my first surf in February '08 at age – let's call it 30-something – I had to kick myself and question why it had never really crossed my mind before. I just loved it! I'm a bit obsessive by nature and go full-throttle with passion and enthusiasm in everything I do, so I booked a surf lesson, bought the rashie, the springie (I can call it that now!) and the board.

During my first five weeks surfing I had one bluebottle sting, one infected leg, three black eyes and probably close to 50 bruises. Then there was the 5000 litres of water which ventured up my nose, the snapped board, the two new boards, the dalliances with several cute boys (you know who you are) and a hell of a lot of fun!

Aside from the sheer fun of being out on the waves (hopefully on top of them more than underneath them), I have been blown away by the surfing community. It's as if I've been ushered into a secret world I never knew existed, a world where people chill out a million miles away from their crazy fast-paced lives onshore, not caring what they look like or how they perform. It doesn't get much better than that.

I love Australia and the outdoors, our hot tourism spots, and our people, and my team and I are proud to produce a series of books that reflect the amazing spirit of Australia.

We're pleased to be supporting a host of surfing organisations and charities plus all the councils and the local community organisations featured in this book, Surfing Australia, Surfing NSW, local surf schools, Surf Life Saving Australia, Barton Lynch's The Surfer's Group, and the list goes on ...

I hope you fall in love with surfing as much as I have! See you out there.

Lisa, CEO Messenger Publishing

Lisa x

Welcome to
Bo

Welcome to

Bondi Beach *(pronounced bond-eye)* is as Australian as the meat pie or the kangaroo. It's one of our most famous icons, drawing thousands of locals and visitors to its gorgeous breaking shore every year. Ask any local and they'll say the same thing – Bondi is more than just a beach. It's a melting pot of everything surf and sand, filled with people of all ages and ethnicities, all coming together to enjoy the sand on their feet, the breeze on their face and the waves on their bodies. A stroll along the promenade or beach showcases the famous swimming and surfing, the array of great food and coffee, and all those funky clubs and pubs. There's nothing better than an afternoon spent people-watching, checking out all the characters in the neighborhood. From dog walkers to yoga enthusiasts, joggers to topless sunbakers and even the odd kite flier, Bondi has it all.

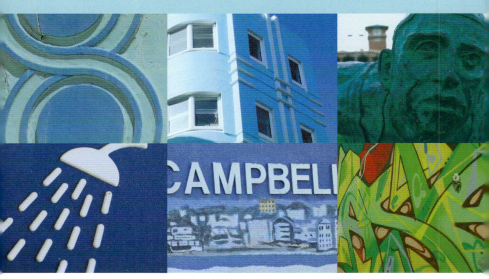

Bondi Beach!

Bondi Beach became a public beach in 1882. The home of the famous Icebergs – historic baths and poolside complex – plays host to many cultural events each year, including the annual City to Surf footrace, Australia's premier short film festival Flickerfest, the amazing annual Sculpture by the Sea exhibition, and even the 2000 Sydney Olympics beach volleyball tournaments. Locals are proud of their home, and its infamous Backpacker Rip that can land surfers two beaches over – or so they say!

Here we kick into the surfing info specific to Bondi Beach before moving on to look at more general learn-to-surf tips and techniques. For more information on Bondi Beach itself, flip to the second section of this guide, where you'll find everything from the history of this idyllic place to the best clubs and restaurants to visit.

Snapshot

Population: 10,373
Currency: AUD, A$
Electricity: 220–240V 50Hz
International dialling code: + 61
Weights and measures: Metric
Language: English

Quick overview

- Bondi is located on the east coast of Australia, 7 km east of the Sydney city centre.

- The name 'Bondi' comes from an Aboriginal word meaning 'noise of water breaking over rocks'.

- The actual beach is roughly 1 km long, faces south and hosts up to 40,000 visitors a day during summer.

- The beach is patrolled seven days a week by a combination of paid lifeguards, surf life saving club members and its mass of surfers.

- The beach is 50 m wide at the northern end and 100 m wide at the southern end.

- On average, the water is 21 degrees in summer and 16 degrees in winter.

- There is a shark net laid 150 m from the beach, set in 8 m of water – although there hasn't been a shark fatality at Bondi since 1937.

Location

Bondi – the beach and the suburb – is located 7 km east of Sydney, New South Wales, or 33°53'20" south 151°16'24" east. It's about 15 minutes drive from the CBD and the Sydney airport and nearby suburbs include Bronte, Waverley and Bondi Junction.

Bondi Beach

History

- When Europeans first colonised the area, Bondi was overlooked as nothing more than a huge sand dune (shame on them)!

- It became a public beach in 1882 but bathing was banned there until 1906.

- During World War II, the beach was actually shelled by a Japanese submarine, but fortunately damage was minimal.

- 6 February 1938 is considered one of the darkest days Bondi Beach has ever seen, when 300 swimmers were swept out to sea by three enormous waves and a strong rip current. Sunbathers quickly morphed into volunteers, and more than 80 impromptu lifesavers rescued all but five of the 300 drowning swimmers. The anniversary is now called 'Black Sunday'.

Interesting facts

- It is estimated that 2.5 million people visit Bondi Beach every year.

- There are roughly 2900 rescues on Bondi Beach every year, carried out by lifeguards and surf life saving volunteers. There are double the rescues at South Bondi than there are at North Bondi (which is why all the families head north!).

- Up until the mid-1990s, an untreated sewage outlet drained into the ocean not far from the north end of Bondi Beach. The sewer inspired the term 'Bondi Cigar' that locals used to somewhat mockingly refer to the human faeces that could sometimes be found floating in on the tide. Thankfully that's all in the past.

- Bondi has been the setting for at least three Australian television dramas, including *Bondi Rescue*, *The Block* and *Breakers* plus a 1959 film.

Surfing at Bondi

While Bondi might not create the biggest and best surfing waves in Australia, it certainly creates one of the best surfing cultures to be found anywhere. The beach and promenade is alive with surfers all year round, from the tanned boardshort-wearing crew of summer to the full kitted-up guys and girls braving the cooler temperatures in winter.

With Bondi's history of surfing and surf life saving going back to the early 1900s, Bondi Beach is a premier surfing spot for beginners and experienced riders alike, thanks to a variety of waves along the 1 km beach.

The beach is split into two main areas – North Bondi, the perfect arena for beginner surfers due to the protection that the Ben Buckler headland provides, and South Bondi, the territory of the more experienced surfers. The middle section is usually for swimming and, heading back from the water, it's also where you'll find food to nibble on, the lifeguard tower and the Bondi Pavilion, the cultural meeting place of Bondi for shows, exhibitions and community events.

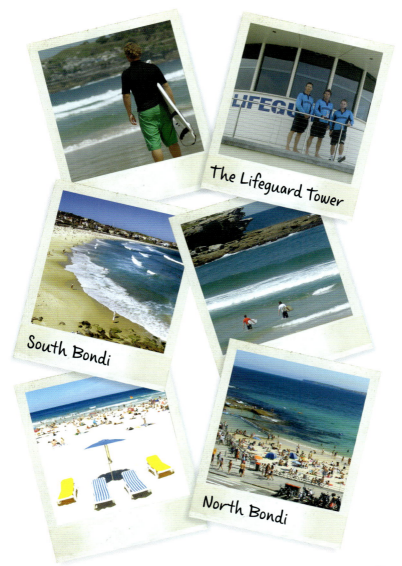

The Lifeguard Tower

South Bondi

North Bondi

Bondi from the air

Bondi Pavilion

Lifeguard Tower

South Bondi

Backpackers R
(is usually around her

Icebergs
Bondi Baths

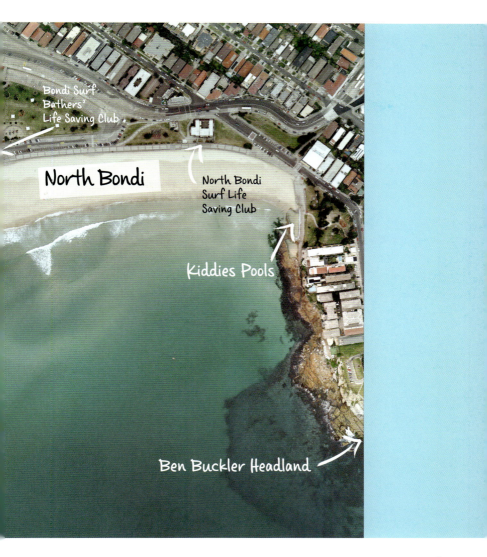

Bondi Surf Bathers' Life Saving Club

North Bondi

North Bondi Surf Life Saving Club

Kiddies Pools

Ben Buckler Headland

North and south

North Bondi: Protected by the Ben Buckler headland, the waves at North Bondi usually form a continuous attached bar cut by one to two rips. There's a permanent rip flowing next to the northern rock pool. Because of the protection from the headland, there is always some sort of wave at this beach. Locals say you can surf 98 days out of 100 here – which is not a bad statistic! Generally, North Bondi is the place for beginner surfers (on soft boards only – see rules of the beach below) and for families. To the locals, it's known as 'kiddies corner', and it also houses the paddling pools, the Wally Weekes Pool and the Children's Wading Pool.

South Bondi: This is where you'll find the more experienced surfers. Being more exposed and with a continuous bar cut by two to three rips, it creates better opportunities for more powerful manoeuvres. This area is often separated from the shore by a longshore trough and, with a persistent large and fairly strong rip running against the southern headland, it provides more excitement on the waves, but greater hazards for the less experienced surfer. Generally speaking, South Bondi is for surfers, but it also enjoys a large backpacker contingent because of its close proximity to most of Bondi's backpacker accommodation. It also houses the famous Bondi Baths, which are more than 100 years old.

BONDI ROAD
Bondi Beach ↑

Best conditions

Waves are pumping the biggest and best with a south swell and a north, north-west wind, and the best time to jump is mid-tide on the rise. For beginners, though, north-easterly offshore winds are best, producing a glassy smooth surface and smaller waves. Bondi enjoys a mix of ground and wind swells and produces right- and left-handers. The main dangers are rocks (mainly down south) ... and the crowds.

Rips and dangers

On any given day there are multiple rips operating at Bondi. While these change and move around, there are two rips that are constant – the Backpackers Rip in the south and one that runs along the rocks in the north. Wherever you have a headland or rocks, there will always be some sort of drag rip running along it. Watch for lifeguard boards stationed on the beach. Any sitting up on their side and facing the water indicate that there is a rip directly in front of it.

Local intel: Bluebottles

In easterly weather and with an onshore breeze, Bondi can be littered with bluebottles, little stingers that do just that – sting like crazy. There's more info on these guys and what to do when you get stung later on.

When the wind is blowing north-east, bluebottles tend to be swept to Bronte Beach instead, and Bondi escapes the onslaught.

The 'Backpackers Rip'

Also known as the 'Backpackers Express',
the 'Bondi Tram' or the 'Bronte Express' ...

A Bondi local, this rip has been known to take tourists all the way to Bronte. Okay, so maybe not quite that far.

'We call it the Backpackers Rip because they are the ones that usually get caught in it,' says Bondi lifeguard and former pro surfer Rod Kerr. 'It's always down south just in front of the pool and because that's where most of the hostels are, they just tend to wander down and set up camp there. But they don't realise it's the most powerful part of the beach and not everyone can swim there. It's often not long before they're in the water yelling for help. The actual rip moves around a bit, but from day to day, it never moves more than 100 m up and down the beach.'

Rules of the beach

Patrolled: Bondi is a patrolled beach every day of the year. There is a central lifeguard tower that is always manned and you will find volunteer lifesavers in red and yellow along the beach. There are usually two other portable manned towers. Lifeguards are onsite from 8 am to 5 pm from May to September, from 6 am to 6 pm from late September to late October (the start of daylight savings), from 6 am to 7 pm from late October to early March, and from 6 am to 6 pm in April.

Flags: In summer there are two sets of red and yellow flags which indicate safe swimming areas. In winter, there is only one set of flags.

Hard board surfing: You are not allowed to surf between the flags if you are riding a hard board. You are allowed into this designated swimming area, though, if you are using a soft board. Generally speaking, hard board riders stay at least 100 m to the right and left of the flags to ensure they don't accidentally ride a wave into swimmers and whack them in the head with an out of control board.

Summer surfing: In summer, watch for No Surfing signs at North Bondi. You will find that surfers with hard boards will almost always be directed to South Bondi during summer. You can surf North Bondi with a soft board.

Alternatives: Surfers, swimmers and beachgoers are given alternatives and with both lifeguard posts and signs being portable, depending on the conditions, keep a lookout for signs that indicate safe swimming and/or surfing or no swimming and/or surfing.

Need help: If you find yourself in trouble in the water, simply raise one arm to attract attention and keep it raised until you are certain a lifeguard or someone else is coming to help.

Surf clubs: The Bondi Surf Bathers' Life Saving Club was founded in 1904 and is said to be the nation's oldest. The present club house was opened in 1934. The North Bondi Surf Club was also founded in 1907 and the present club opened in 1932.

Bondi Beach

SHALLOW WATER

HIGH SURF

DANGEROUS CURRENT

SHORE DUMP

LIFE SAVING SERVICES

PLEASE SWIM ONLY BETWEEN
THE RED AND YELLOW FLAGS
This beach is patrolled where the
red & yellow flags are displayed

REGULATIONS

Rod Kerr

Bondi lifeguard, Bondi Rescue regular and former pro surfer Rod Kerr caught his first wave at the age of five. He went on to win national surfing titles and compete on the world tour for 12 years before he settled into the lifeguard tower at Bondi Beach. We caught up with him for a chat about surfing, rescues and life in the lifeguard's tower.

"We'd sit and talk to people all day about Bondi and the beach if they asked. Our tower is always open."

First wave: I was about five and it was over here at Bronte.

What I love about surfing: Being out there in the water, on your own or with mates ... it's like no other feeling.

Surfing career: I really hate talking about this stuff (laughs). I had a pretty good amateur career and won a fair few Australian titles. I went on the tour and made the top 44. I was on the tour for 12 years. Competing was hard because you were travelling with your mates and competing with your mates. You're fighting for the waves and to be the best; it became a bit of a chore after a while. Now it's about pure enjoyment.

Favourite surf spot: Fiji is unbelievable and one of the best spots. It's paradise, close to home and relatively cheap and of course, the surf there is incredible.

Beach stats: There are 2.5 million people on average who come to Bondi Beach each year and we do about 2500 rescues. The surf life saving guys do a few hundred on top of that so it's a lot.

Always watching: We're always watching and we know where each other is looking. I might be talking to you now but I'm watching over this side and they're watching the other. If we get up and leave you know something has happened.

The flags: We do our best to keep people swimming between the flags but we can only advise people, we can't enforce it. We do our best to look after everyone and to make sure everyone gets to share the beach and the water.

Talk Bondi: We'd sit and talk to people all day about Bondi and the beach if they asked. Our tower is always open.

Worst surfing accident or injury at Bondi: It would have to be drowning which is horrible to talk about but it does happen. We had an incident where a young girl went under during a wave and we just saw her board pop up. We sent the guys out and they dragged her in and we managed to revive her which was fortunate. We get a lot of spinal injuries here as well, mainly from people nose-diving into the sand. Then there are dislocated shoulders, cuts, fin chops and boards flying into people's faces.

Your worst surfing injury: I cracked a vertebra in my back and I've had knee surgery.

Advice for beginner surfers: Keep trying and keep getting out there. It's like anything, you'll have some good days and some really bad ones, especially because surfing is so difficult. One good wave or manoeuvre will make your day and keep you hungry for more. You are always one wave away from having the best surf of your life.

Advice on rips: Don't be afraid of them. If you're on a patrolled beach like Bondi, look for the dangerous current signs or the surfboard markings because 99.9 per cent of times, the rips are near those signs. If you get in one unintentionally, don't panic, just paddle (or swim) parallel to the beach and guaranteed you will eventually pop out of it.

Unwritten rule: Never surf alone. If you hurt yourself or something happens, you want someone there to keep an eye on you. It's more important for isolated areas.

Look out for others: If you see someone in trouble, a swimmer or surfer, paddle over there and help them. This is another unwritten surfing rule. Drag them onto your board and then wash in together. If you're on a patrolled beach, grab a lifeguard or try and get their attention.

Localism at Bondi: It used to be a pretty big thing here, but we have so many tourists now and people from all over Sydney here that localism has pretty much gone. You'll go and surf three or four days in a row and only know one or two people. A few years ago you would have known everyone. There are spots along the beach where people tend to congregate – like families up north and backpackers and tourist down south – but in terms of the nasty tribalism you hear of in other more isolated beaches, you won't find it here.

Rod's colleagues at the Lifeguard Tower

Nearby breaks

There's more info on these places later and how to get to them, but in short, Bondi has breaks all around it! Tamarama is just 1 km away, a tiny beach with a left-hand reef break that's best in a south-west wind. McKenzies Bay is also 1 km away, an exposed beach break that's best with a south swell and a north wind. Bronte Beach (pictured), 2 km down the road, is a popular beach but has inconsistent surf. It's best in a south-east swell and west wind and offers left-handers from the beach and right-handers from the reef. Clovelly (3 km away) is a popular spot for beach goers and, when it's cranking, for surfers. Best in west winds with an east, north-east swell. Coogee (4 km away) has inconsistent surf that is best with a westerly wind and a south-east swell. Offers left- and right-hand beach and reef breaks.

Tips for Bondi learners

From Brenda Miley
of Let's Go Surfing Bondi

1. Get the right equipment and use the right equipment.

2. Get a lesson. It takes years to learn how to surf, so getting some advice can help you form good habits and fast track your success.

3. For Bondi, begin at the northern end of the beach where the waves are gentler and break into 'fatter' water.

4. Start in the white water so you can practise your skills while being able to put your feet down as well.

5. Understand and respect the ocean.

6. Know the rules of the beach and respect the locals.

Brenda Miley

Bondi's Brenda Miley helped put female surfing on the map. She rode her first wave at the age of three (courtesy of her dad's back) and by 10 was in love with the sport. Since then, the former physical education teacher has surfed on almost every continent, has competed in the Australian Women's Surf Titles and has been involved in a stack of surfing bodies, from starting the Bondi Girls Surfriders Club to being the Women's Director for Surfing Australia. Brenda started her surf lesson business Lets Go Surfing from the back of a van when the sport was still considered 'uncool', and today teaches thousands of visitors to Bondi how to make it in the waves.

It all began: I started surfing at about 10 at Tamarama Beach. I don't remember thinking it was too big or anything, but Tama is actually considered one of the most dangerous beaches in Australia to swim and surf at.

Out of control: I love the way surfing makes you feel. It's the freedom, the fun, the adventure, the fitness. You're out in nature. You're not in control and I love that.

Uncool: I never told anyone that I surfed. It wasn't something that was cool. Nowadays, surfing is so cool that people say they surf even if they don't.

Bondi Beach: Bondi is a melting pot of so many different sorts of people. As a culture, it is more generous than most, particularly because the beach is so busy at times. We're all used to lots of tourists and visitors from other parts of Sydney so we've become an 'anything goes' beach. It's this diversity that adds the element of excitement and fun because there's always something happening here. The people who live here love it.

Girls and surfing: Female surfing has come a long way. When I started, there were no female wetsuits or rashies or anything. It was a boys' club. And while there's still some way to go, as a general rule, female surfers are now embraced by the wider surfing community. I've been a big advocate for female surfing, having spent most of my early days out there with the boys. While it toughened me up, it was always nice to see other girls in the water.

"I love the way surfing makes you feel. It's the freedom, the fun, the adventure, the fitness. You're out in nature. You're not in control and I love that."

Brenda
Miley

"Female surfing has come a long way. When I started, there were no female wetsuits or rashies or anything. It was a boys' club."

Tips for girls riding the waves:

1. Make sure you stay safe and know your limitations. What's big to you may not be big to a guy so bear that in mind.

2. Don't get out of your comfort zone until you are ready.

3. Don't be intimated by boys in the surf. They generally like the fact that you're out there and they are definitely not as scary as you think.

4. Say 'hi' to other girls that are out there and join clubs so you can go on the surfing journey together.

Tips for Bondi learners

1. Get the right equipment and use the right equipment.

2. Take a lesson. It takes years to learn how to surf so getting some advice can help you form good habits and fast-track your success.

3. For Bondi, begin at the northern end of the beach where the waves are gentler and breaks into 'fatter' water.

4. Start in the white water so you can practise your skills while being able to put your feet down as well.

5. Understand and respect the ocean.

6. Know the rules of the beach and respect the locals.

Overcoming fear: Once you've hurt yourself, overcoming fear is a difficult thing and few people acknowledge that. If you're starting out, don't let your first real wipeout or being caught in a rip or even getting stuck on a massive wave stop you from surfing. Go back to what you were comfortable doing, such as surfing in the whitewater, or whatever it is, and regain your confidence step by step. But you've got to always get back on the horse, get straight back in there and try again.

Dave Hannagan, commonly known as 'Big Wave Dave', surfs the local breaks every morning before spending his days teaching others to do the same. We caught up with him for the lowdown on surfing and Bondi ...

Surfing: Surfing is a lifestyle. It's like a religion or a drug, it's addictive. If you haven't been surfing for a while or the surf hasn't been good, you start to feel a little bit depressed. It's an excellent way to stay fit and every wave is different. No two waves in the world are ever the same which makes it a challenging sport to learn, both physically and mentally.

Surfing in Australia: Thirty years ago there were no instructors, everyone just learnt by watching others. These days people can do a surf course and after about six to 10 hours of tuition, they are up and standing, learning how to turn and move on a wave.

Bondi: I moved here 15 years ago because I read in a magazine they needed a Japanese-speaking instructor. It was an excellent decision because Bondi is a great place to live and surf. It's great for teaching because of its southern exposure and bay-like beach. It's protected from the onshore winds and we don't get too many bluebottles and other things like that.

Funny sights: You always see people coming down here trying to teach themselves to surf and they have their wetsuit on back-to-front and the leg rope is on their wrist. They are trying to surf in the most dangerous, rippy areas, lying on the very back of the board with no hope of catching a wave, basically making the sport look really uncool.

Dave's top two tips: 1. Driving the right vehicle for the right stage of your journey is key. Get something that's big and long at first. A shortboard is two years down the track. Surfing is hard enough as it is. 2. Get lessons from a professional instructor.

Big Wave Dave is a surf instructor with Lets Go Surfing Bondi.

Big Wave Dave

1.

So, you

SU

want to

RF

RESPECT (of the ocean and its power, and of other surfers)

COURAGE (to tackle that first wave and every one thereafter)

PERSEVERANCE (you will get knocked down … over and over)

COURTESY (make friends out there, not enemies)

SOME KNOWLEDGE (read on … surfing is a great pastime if you know a thing or two)

N'T

start without

A short history
of surfing

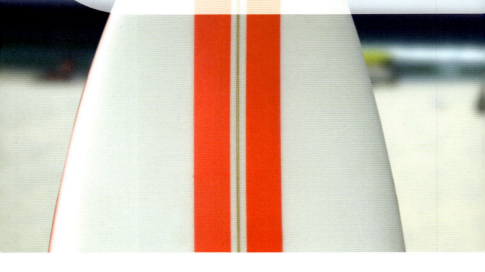

Under Hawaiian law, if a man and woman rode a wave together, they were permitted to get down and dirty in the sand once ashore. But it wasn't all sexy summer lovin' for the common folk. If a rank and file surfer was caught riding an olo board – the very long boards carved out of single slabs of the precious wili wili or koa wood and reserved for Hawaiian royalty – they would be ritually decapitated in ceremonies overseen by a kahuna (a medicine-man).

Puts a whole fresh slant on dying to go surfing, doesn't it? In fact, despite thoroughbred horse racing being commonly referred to as 'the sport of kings', in Hawaiian culture for a long time, surfing truly was a sport reserved for kings.

But then ... that puts you in good company!

Seems CRAZY ...

Between 1962 and 1968 surfers in Sydney were forced to register their boards or fear losing them. Permits were purchased from local councils 'for a couple of pound, from memory,' recalls Mark Windon from Surfing NSW – in response to public safety concerns. Valid only for beaches in that council area, some surfers were sporting two to three validation stickers per board. While the permits were considered ridiculous at the time, boards with permit stickers are now considered a collector's item and can fetch in excess of $3000.

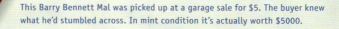

This Barry Bennett Mal was picked up at a garage sale for $5. The buyer knew what he'd stumbled across. In mint condition it's actually worth $5000.

15th century

Hawaiian islanders perfect the art of surfing – turning the pastime into one of the pillars of island society and religion.

1778

Captain Cook and his crew become the first Europeans to visit the Hawaiian Islands. After observing hundreds of locals surfing at Kealakekua Bay on the Big Island, members of the ship's crew produce the first written account of the sport.

1820

Calvinist missionaries from Boston, Massachusetts settle on the Hawaiian Islands. In the following hundred years, the missionaries put a halt to all traditional island pastimes that comprised the Hawaiian culture – including gambling, casual sex, playing in the ocean, and surfing.

1907

Jack London publishes the book *The Cruise of the Snark* after spending over two years on his sailboat in the South Pacific. The chapter entitled 'A Royal Sport: Surfing in Waikiki' generates international interest in surfing and helps to keep the dying Hawaiian surf culture alive.

1909

West Pictures produces Surf Sports at Manly – the first newsreel in a series of documentaries spotlighting the importance of the ocean in Australian culture.

1912

The first surfboard arrives in Australia – a four-metre 'alaia' makes the long journey from Hawaii in the luggage of Manly resident CD Paterson. Legend says CD didn't master the surf so he gave it to his mother to use as an ironing board.

December 1914

Bronzed beauty, Olympic swimmer ... and of course, great surfer, Duke Kahanamoku, is invited by the NSW Swimming Association to give a public swimming demonstration at Manly's Freshwater Beach. Instead, he grabs local teenager Elizabeth Latham, throws her on a board, and shows Aussies how to surf – on a board he hand-carved out of a raw slab of local sugar pine.

1935

Early design genius and pioneering waterman Tom Blake is the first person to plonk a fin on a surfboard. Blake was responsible for several design revolutions during his truly fascinating life, including building and patenting the first hollow surfboard and paddleboard, making the first sailboard, and basically creating the template for the surfer lifestyle we all emulate to this day.

1946

The first fibreglass surfboard built.

1922

The Royal Lifesaving Society unites with local lifesaving clubs to form the Surf Life Saving Association of Australia.

1946

Californian dentist and legendary surf photographer Doc Ball publishes *California Surfriders*, arguably the best photography book about early surfing.

1947

Greg 'Da Bull' Noll along with Dale 'The Hawk' Velzy and the Manhattan Beach Surf Club revolutionise surf culture abroad, changing the social image of the surfer and inventing the first pair of 'surf trunks' – a pair of white sailor pants from the local military surplus store torn off around the knees. Alas, the boardie was born.

Circa 1948–53

A crew of surfers at Malibu in Los Angeles, including board shapers Joe Quig and Matt Kivlin, pioneer the first lightweight balsawood and fibreglass surfboards. They had improved upon the groundbreaking work of eccentric genius Bob Simmons, who had earlier built hybrid boards from fibreglass, timber and foam. These boards are still called Malibus or 'mals' today after their Malibu birthplace.

Circa 1950

Californian surfers invent the skateboard as a means of surfing on land.

1953

Bud Browne popularises surfing culture with Hawaiian Surfing Movie, the first commercial surf film to be shown to the general public.

1956

A crew of Californian lifeguards, in Australia as part of the US Olympic team for the 1956 Melbourne games, introduce balsa and fibreglass surfboards to the Australian public. The Yanks, including future big wave hero Greg Noll and all-time great waterman Tommy Zahn, bombed in the official events they entered but their legacy to Aussie surfers cannot be underestimated. The locals had been stuck in surfing's dark ages, 'riding' 16 to 18 foot long hollow timber boards known as toothpicks. The Californians' mastery of their 10 foot longboard showed what was possible and Aussie surfing was launched into the jet age in full, living Technicolour. The genie was well and truly out of the bottle!

1957

A group of Californian surfers, including Greg Noll, Pat Curran and Mickey Munoz ride big-wave spot Waimea Bay for the first time. The venue will remain area zero for big wave performance surfing for the next 40 years.

1957

The novel Gidget, written by Jewish émigré and Hollywood scriptwriter Frederick Kohner, is published and becomes a massive bestseller. Based on his daughter Katherine's summer experience learning to surf at the then pristine and uncrowded Malibu, the surprisingly perceptive novel inspired a film version in 1959. It was this event more than any other that blew doors off what was essentially a bohemian pastime with a cult following, and changed surfing forever. Within a year Hollywood was pumping out surf themed B-films and surf gear was being hustled across the landlocked states of America. Some surfers have never forgiven the Gidge ... but without her, you wouldn't be reading this book, would you?

1958

The first lightweight foam and fibreglass surfboards are built, replacing the heavier and increasingly hard to source balsawood. These space-age 'sticks' are so easy to manufacture that they become the conduit for the surf culture explosion of the next decade.

1960

Photographer and filmmaker John Severson publishes the first surfing magazine, Surfer. It was initially created purely as a one-off to promote his latest surf film, but Surfer quickly establishes itself as the first bible of surfing and inspires a pack of competitors. Surf culture and surfers' view of themselves would never be the same.

1962

The inaugural Bell's Beach Easter contest is held near Torquay, Victoria in Australia. The event later becomes the Rip Curl Pro and is one of the longest-running pro events in existence.

1964

The first world championship is held at Sydney's Manly Beach. Local lad Midget Farrelly is crowned male champ and Queenslander Phyllis O'Donnell the female champ. This was a precursor to the professional world championships, which would not begin until 1976.

1964

Californian kneeboarder and eccentric George Greenough meets Aussie surfboard shaper Bob McTavish while visiting Australia. The two combine ideas and change surfboard design theorems forever, creating the first functional shortboard. Californian Jim Foley had championed shorter boards, known as Foley boards, before then, but these were essentially scaled down longboard designs. McTavish and Greenough, on the other hand, made radical experimentation with design their mantra.

1967

Bob McTavish and Nat Young show off their new sub-8 foot long Keyo 'Plastic Machine' boards in Hawaii at the Duke Kahanamoku Invitational. The radically wide, thinner, flexible-finned and deep V-bottomed boards performed poorly at the contest at Sunset Beach. But later, in the perfect 10 foot surf of Maui's Honolua Bay, they announce the vanguard of a new world order. The shortboard revolution has officially begun.

1971

The leg rope appears on the scene for board control and safety – pushing previous performance boundaries, increasing the number of surfers in the water, and forever changing the art of surfing.

Circa 1974-6

Future world champion Mark Richards begins experimenting with twin-fin surfboards. These brea‹through designs will spur him on to four world titles and inspire legions of surfers to ride increasingly sophisticated equipment.

1976

The first professional world tour is created, with Aussie Peter Townend named the very first pro surfing world champion.

1981

Australian pro surfer and surfboard designer Simon Anderson gifts the world his three-finned design, the 'Thruster'. A fine tuning of previous three-finned boards such as the 'Bonzer', Anderson quells any doubt as to the 'Thruster's' worth by cleaning up the big contests that year on boards he had shaped himself.

1983

The first Triple Crown of Surfing takes place along Oahu's North Shore, destined to become the ultimate test of courage and skill for professional surfers.

1983

Australia's Tom Carroll wins his first world championship while riding a tri-fin set-up.

Circa 1991

Big wave surfing is reinvigorated and revolutionised, with jet skis towing surfers further out into previously unobtainable waves.

1992

Huntington Beach's Joey Hawkins brings the Oxbow World Longboard Championship to California, revitalising the popularity of the longboard.

Our
WORLD CHAMPS

Aussie men

1964 Midget Farrelly
1966 Nat Young
1970 Nat Young
1972 Paul Neilsen
1973 Ian Cairns
1975 Mark Richards
1976 Peter Townend
1978 Wayne Bartholomew
1979 Mark Richards
1980 Mark Richards
1981 Mark Richards
1982 Mark Richards
1983 Tom Carroll
1984 Tom Carroll
1987 Damien Hardman
1988 Barton Lynch
1991 Damien Hardman
1999 Mark Occhilupo
2007 Mick Fanning

Aussie women

1964 Phyllis O'Donnell
1989 Wendy Botha
1990 Pam Burridge
1991 Wendy Botha
1992 Wendy Botha
1993 Pauline Menczer
1998 Layne Beachley
1999 Layne Beachley
2000 Layne Beachley
2001 Layne Beachley
2002 Layne Beachley
2003 Layne Beachley
2005 Chelsea Georgeson
2006 Layne Beachley
2007 Stephanie Gilmore

Aussie longboarding men

1986 Nat Young
1987 Stuart Entwistle
1988 Nat Young
1989 Nat Young
1990 Nat Young
1991 Martin McMillan
2000 Beau Young
2003 Beau Young
2006 Josh Constable

Layne Beachley

Statistically the greatest female surfer to walk the face of the earth, Layne Beachley has won seven world titles, six of them in a row, and has the female record for riding the largest wave (over 15 m). By the age of 20, she was already sixth in the world and the Manly local was on her way to surfing glory. Today she continues to be passionate about the sport and, in particular, the progression of women's surfing.

Early days: I started

skateboarding when I was three so it was a natural progression to go from the land to the water. I guess I was about four. I grew up around the beaches of Manly.

Layne Beachley

Ambitions: I wanted to be a professional tennis player. I never planned to make surfing into a career. There wasn't much support for women's surfing back then so I didn't consider it a viable option. It was just something that I always loved.

Change: Not only have the numbers increased but the ability of surfers has improved dramatically, especially in the last five to 10 years. When I was growing up I was the only girl out. I'd come home from being on tour and there was no support there. No one was making women's surf gear, but now it's a multibillion dollar industry of surf schools and clothing. Kids are getting picked up when they're still teenagers and being paid hundreds of thousands of dollars before they've even shown that they have the ability to win. When I was 20, I was trying to take on the world on just $8000 a year. I would love to be starting out now.

First win: The ultimate event win for me was my first one in '93 at North Narrabeen because it instilled the confidence in me to believe that I was capable of winning events and that told me that I was capable of winning world titles as well.

"There wasn't much support for women's surfing back then so I didn't consider it a viable option. It was just something that I always loved."

A great moment: The final of the Roxy Pro in 2000 when Lisa Anderson came back from 18 months off and was in the final with me. She was beating me in the last 10 seconds and that was hard to take because the American media were saying I had only won two world titles because of her absence from the tour. [Then in those last few moments], a wave presented itself and I just surfed with so much anger and I won it on that wave. That was quite an emotional victory and a satisfying one.

Injuries: Yeah, many, it's easiest to work my way down. I had a herniated disc in my neck severing 80 per cent of my spinal cord from a wipeout, 10 stitches in my cheek in Japan which left me with a smile line (that's a very painful way to get a dimple), a fractured rib after being back-slammed by a contestant, torn ligaments and meniscus in both knees, and a lumbar spine injury crushed several of my vertebrae after a wave landed in the middle of my lower back and bent it so my toes touched my head. They are probably my worst.

Advice for beginners: Be patient because it's not as easy as we make it look. Also, go to a surf school to learn proper technique because I taught myself to surf and it took me a long time to correct the bad techniques I had created.

Respect: You need to respect the ocean because it mirrors or reflects your emotions. If you paddle out there feeling arrogant or cocky, it will kick your arse.

On your own: I surf every day for myself for at least half an hour. Sometimes I have to put it in my diary just to make sure I find time to do it.

Surfing love: I love how it rinses my soul every time I dive into the water. I also love the freedom of expression and the individuality it allows me to experience out there.

Styles of
SUR

There are two main surfing styles, longboarding and shortboarding. In simple terms, longboards are easier for beginners to manage, while shortboards offer more scope for manoeuvrability. There's more to it than that, though – the different boards also offer up very different surfing experiences.

FING

Longboard surfing is the classically cool, Hawaiian/Californian way of surfing that's all about grace and style. (Can you hear the tropical music beginning to play and see the Polynesian girl with a hibiscus flower in her hair slowly riding to the shore?) When you longboard, you ride a huge board, your turns are slow and graceful and, as many surfers say, 'uncluttered'. Or as THE original surf hero of the 1950s and '60s, Californian Phil Edwards said, longboards are about 'making the difficult look easy'. Nice challenge that!

Longboarding has been around since the beginning of surfing but after a decline in the late 1960s when the shortboard boom began, it developed a new cult following in the 1990s. After suffering ridicule for decades, the longboard was cool again, and hasn't looked back since.

Boards are long and wide. Traditional styles have just one fin to keep turns slow and graceful. They were originally up to 24 foot long, and made from solid wood, but these days they are much lighter, made from foam and fibreglass, and are typically capped at 12 foot long.

Longboarding

Shortboarding

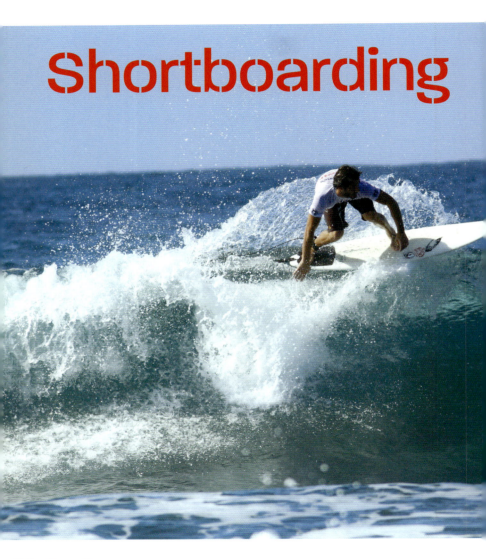

Shortboard surfing is all about quick turns, critical positioning and aggressive moves. With a shortboard you have freedom to change direction in an instant, ride inside the barrel of waves, and have a seriously damn good time – but you have to be quick and you need pretty good balance.

Many people start on a longboard and then venture up to a shortboard if they want some more action. The 'shortboard revolution', as it's called, happened in the mid to late 1960s when many surfers literally cut down and reshaped the ends of their boards to a point so they could move faster and with more freedom.

Australians were a key part of this revolution after Aussie Nat Young won the World Championships in 1966 on a 9 foot, 4 inch board (which at the time was considered pretty short!). After that, the experimenting began, and plenty of it on our shores. A lot of this included tinkering with certain mind-altering substances that inspired some truly weird and horrible boards; but hey, it was during the hippie years, so it's understandable. During this time, boards dropped from the usual 10 feet to 7 feet (or even shorter) and grew from one fin to two and then three.

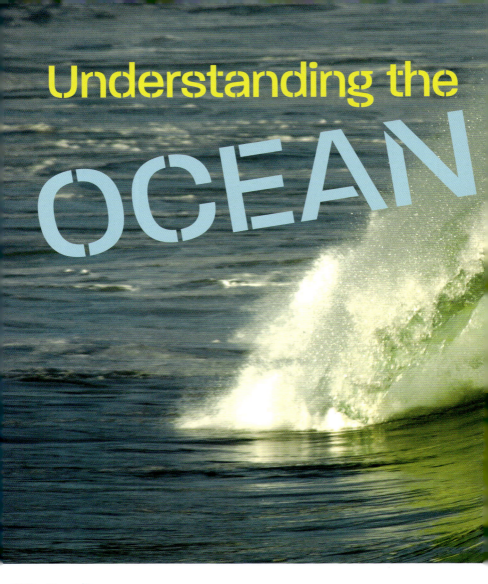

Understanding the
OCEAN

If you don't know too much about the ocean, here's a quick lesson. It's super-important for surfers to have at least a basic understanding of the relationship between the wind, the water and the waves — for awareness, and also for safety. Actually, it's pretty cool how it all works.

How WAVES are created

Winds out to sea cause masses of energy to disperse through the water, a similar scenario to when you drop a rock into a pool of water and watch the ripples it creates. As this energy passes through larger expanses of water (think continent to continent), gorgeous, consistent and more uniform swell is created. When this swell meets the shallow ocean floor of our coastlines or reefs, the water slows down and pushes upwards, and – because it has nowhere else to go – waves are created for our surfing and swimming pleasure.

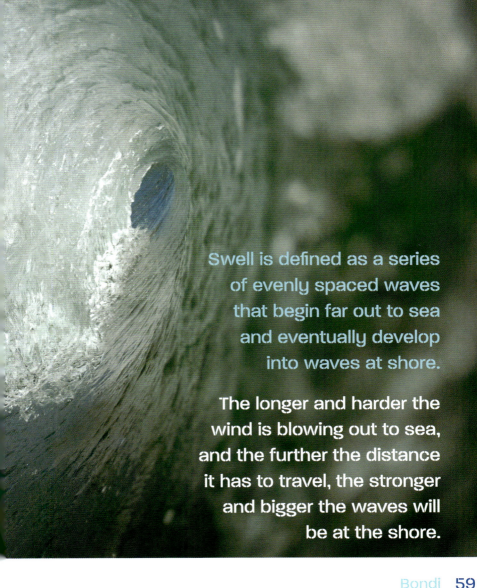

Swell is defined as a series of evenly spaced waves that begin far out to sea and eventually develop into waves at shore.

The longer and harder the wind is blowing out to sea, and the further the distance it has to travel, the stronger and bigger the waves will be at the shore.

Tom Carroll caught his first wave at six, won his first pro junior title at 15 and his first world title at 22. A legend of the sport, he is known for a radical style with late takeoffs on the big waves and for being one of the first surfers to sign a massive sponsorship deal. Tom eventually won two world titles and three Pipe Masters. Many say Tom's style is still a benchmark for modern surfing.

Intrigue: There was this guy that used to walk past us with a massive surfboard on his head and a towel in between his head and the board. He'd walk up the pathway and over the hill down to the beach and it was a long walk. I used to love watching that guy and thought 'What is that on his head?'

First waves: There was a rubber surf plane that we had but my brother wouldn't let me have a go on it. He always had his hands on the thing and my sister would try and get it for a moment, the competition for it was ruthless so it was tough times. But those few waves were enough to give me a taste and I so got off on that feeling. I was probably about six at the time.

"The interaction between you and the ocean is amazing and you can have that anywhere there's water ... and that in itself is quite special."

Surfing love: The interaction between you and the ocean is amazing and you can have that anywhere there's water ... and that in itself is quite special. It's always available rain, hail or shine, night or day, you can go out and dive into the ocean and feel the waves.

Perfect surf: If I could have a perfect 25 ft peak with sheet glass and not one drop of water out of place, with top to bottom one section, with a nice big face in the next, then back into another top to bottom section going both ways, with maybe a channel in the side, then that would be close. Throw in your best mates with jet skies towing you in and a couple of rogue 35 ft sets to keep you on your toes and that's it I reckon.

"Surfing is now quite a mainstream, normal, 'everyone does it' type of weekend activity. It's for people of all walks of life, guys and girls and all ages with the increase of an older crew out there as well."

Tom Carroll

Favourite spot: I just love being on the Northern Beaches, it's a beautiful place to surf and when I'm there I usually have free time and there's no one bugging me so it's my time and I've got space to myself.

Best surfing deed: Sharing waves. That is one of the best things a surfer can do.

Best competition moment: In 1991 when I was on top of my game. Everything came together and it will be forever a lasting memory.

Change: Surfing is now quite a mainstream, normal, 'everyone does it' type of weekend activity. It's for people of all walks of life, guys and girls and all ages with the increase of an older crew out there as well. It wasn't like this in the 60s and 70s, then it was more a cult type of thing and surfers were pinned down by the broader community. We didn't have a good name and to be a surfer went against the grain. Surfing wasn't even seen as a sport. I'd win a state title and even the national junior title and I'd go back to school and see the basketball team that made it in the local competition on the podium in the assembly and I was brushed aside completely.

Advice for beginners: Keep surfing for the love of it so it comes from the heart. If you're a budding professional, or you're a kid who wants to compete and do really well, there's a path open for you to take. But it has to come from you, it can't come from anyone else.

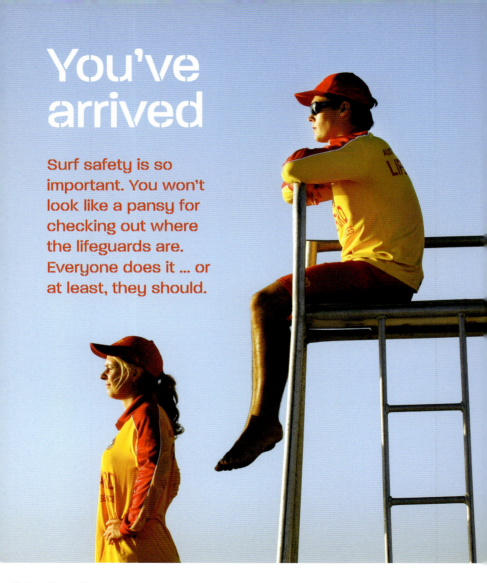

You've arrived

Surf safety is so important. You won't look like a pansy for checking out where the lifeguards are. Everyone does it ... or at least, they should.

Many Australian beaches are patrolled by lifeguards and lifesavers (be aware that uniforms change from beach to beach). It is very important that the first thing you do when arriving at any beach is identify the lifeguards and lifesavers. If you need to find them in an emergency, when time is of the essence, you want to be able to find them very quickly. That's certainly the case in Bondi. When you arrive at the beach, here are a few tips before you begin:

F Find the flags so you know where you can and can't swim and surf.

L Look for safety signs to help you identify potential dangers and daily conditions.

A Ask a lifesaver or lifeguard for advice on surf conditions that day (they won't bite, we promise; in fact most will talk all day).

G Get a friend to surf with you. You should never swim or surf alone.

S Stick your hand up if you get into trouble in the water so a lifesaver, lifeguard or fellow surfer can come to your aid.

Offshore and onshore WINDS

After a while, these two words will become extremely familiar to you, as surfers always talk about the wind being 'onshore' or 'offshore' when they are discussing the surf conditions.

Offshore — when wind is blowing from land to sea. This wind is ideal for surfing as it usually results in a clean wave face that holds up and is beautiful to watch and ride. The sea will generally be glassy, or smooth, and you can see the incoming sets beautifully.

Onshore — when wind is blowing from sea to land. You can still have fun in onshore wind but it is not ideal for surfing, creating a big mess of white water and choppy waves with jumbled swell lines.

Onshore and offshore winds are created because winds cool down and heat up differently when on land and on sea.

Offshore winds

Onshore winds

RIPS – not as scary as you thought

Dye has been purposefully placed in the water to indicate a rip.
(Don't worry, it's an eco-friendly dye).

The bigger the waves the more intense the rips will be, as that water has to go somewhere. A common rip is when water from the incoming waves is draining back out to sea. This can unexpectedly carry people away from the beach and it is the reason why many people drown. More than 70 per cent of rescues are attributed to rips.

Most swimmers avoid rips with vigour, but surfers, lifeguards and lifesavers actually use them to their benefit. It seems weird after years of swimming education and safety training, but if you have a basic understanding of rips, they will become your friend. I heard someone once refer to rips as being like the moving escalators or travelators at airports. They get you to where you want to go, much faster and with less effort.

As you become a more experienced surfer, you'll learn to understand rips and begin to use them.

Rips are currents which form between the shore and sandbars and drain a wave's water back out to sea. Any beach that has incoming waves will experience rips.

Spotting rips

Once you know what to look for, you should be able to sit on the beach and see a rip in the water. Here are a few dead giveaways:

- discoloured or dark water
- calm or still water with waves breaking on either side, and
- foam on the surface at the back of the breaking waves.

And if even if you fail to catch any of these tell-tale signs, most beaches patrolled by lifeguards have large signs showing where the rips are.

PROFILE

Pam Burridge

Pam Burridge started surfing on a homemade board at just 10, won her first state title at 14 and was on the world stage at 17. The self-confessed 'surf rat boy' went on to come runner up in the world titles six times before taking the honours in 1990 by a record number of points. We caught up with Pam to talk about her career, chicks and surfing generally. She now spends her days teaching people to surf.

Competition: I entered my first contest at 12, the Manly Pacific Boardrider's winter point score. When I turned up, before I could say anything, they told me the junior boys was over because I looked like a little surf rat boy. After they discovered I was a girl, I went out there and surfed like crazy. I won a plastic trophy and a T-shirt that was seven sizes too big.

Progression: As soon as I heard you could surf across waves, I did it straight away. I just loved it. I couldn't go backhand for quite a while so I remember the feeling of finally breaking through that first time, and realising that I'd finally done it.

In the line-up: Graduating from kiddies' corner and being flung into the line-up was interesting, suddenly being at the bottom of the pecking order again with all the other groms. I still looked like a boy though so no one really insulted me or gave me the abuse that the other girls were getting at that time.

"I had a level of skill early on so I wasn't so easy to intimidate. But it wasn't very welcoming in a general sense for women at that time on all levels."

Women in the surf: I had a level of skill early on so I wasn't so easy to intimidate. But it wasn't very welcoming in a general sense for women at that time on all levels. There were no wetsuits for women, or boardies for that matter. It was a guy's domain. I had a front-zipper wetsuit that could do a great cleavage shot; it was a ripper. Girls' surf gear really only appeared on the scene in the early 1990s.

Bloopers: I wish I had CCTV for my surf school as I'd win so much money. You see classic wipeouts, you see people paddling backwards and you think 'where did that come from?' People jump on the board facing the wrong way and go 'oh, there's the fin'. I love teaching people though. I don't mind going back to baby sticks. I often go out there and surf switch foot, just to try and feel like a beginner.

Surfing changes: I started competing in '78, '79. When I first started on the pro tour, competitions were actually at better locations (Hawaii and Bells etc), but then through my career it was always beach breaks and pretty crappy waves. Today we are looking at more prime wave events.

The rise of surfing: The whole vibe of surfing has gone ahead in leaps and bounds, but if you dig a little deeper to the competition side, you realise it is the same old thing just with a few more zeroes on the end.

Pro surfing and kids: Professional surfing is pretty brutal. There are a few women who surged to the top of their career but missed out on the opportunity to have a family and that's tough. You can't really be a pro surfer with a family, it's just so hard. Women don't have as many events as the guys – but it's a big sacrifice either way.

Back in the game? People always ask if I'll go back, but we can't now with the kids, it would be too hard. When you see them out there surfing great waves you want to be there. It looks like great fun, but it's not a serious option.

Carpark punch-ups: I run a mile from a fight but I've seen plenty over the surf. In the water, it doesn't last too long, someone just gets held under. I don't like aggression and try to keep away from it. The main problem is people getting in the way and people stealing waves. There are a lot of places learners shouldn't go, but unfortunately sometimes those spots are exactly where they end up and there are not enough waves to go around. My advice is to watch what's going from the beach and once you've earned your stripes, get out there, but not before.

Always learning: We're learners for a very long time. You're always learning something new. There is so much an advanced surfer will know, so watch and learn from them.

Advice for learners: Run your own race and try to target waves that you want to surf. Get in the water as much as you can and try not to let what other people think of you get in the way of what you're trying to do. Don't necessarily go where all the people are.

Advice for aspiring girls: Do a bit more physical training to help with your strength so you can last for more than a couple of waves. We just don't have the basic strength of the blokes, but we are a bit more flexible and we have smaller egos and more tenacity, so that has to count for something!

Favourite surf breaks: Green Island in NSW – the colour of the water on the paddle out is just gorgeous. It's not world class, but the waves are fun and it's just a pretty place. Only a girl would say that!

"There is so much an advanced surfer will know, so watch and learn from them."

Staying safe
in a rip

You can ride the rip out to the back but this is only for experienced swimmers and surfers. As you gradually become more acquainted with the beach and the surf, the rip can become your friend. If you do get caught in a rip unintentionally, don't panic! Don't fight it by trying to paddle to the shore. That will just make you tired and more afraid because you won't get anywhere.

Rips are usually quite narrow. To escape one, move along parallel to the beach until you pop out the other side of it. If you must, ride the rip out into deeper water – it won't carry you off to another country! This is because rips tend to dissipate in deeper water. Then paddle away from the rip while remaining parallel to the beach and catch a wave in to the shore.

Using rips — be experienced!

A quick story about what not to do. I think hanging out with the boys in my first few weeks of surfing was potentially life-threatening! When someone offers me a challenge, I hate to say no, and so I ended up using the rip very early on in my surfing career. In one sense it was great — I was practically catapulted to the back of the break in no time at all.

However, I went out very close to the rocks. Not only that, but I found myself out the back in huge surf, and I really just wasn't ready to be there. Being inexperienced, one false move and I could've ended up in a lot of trouble.

So trust me when I say remember that you don't know what you don't know ... and don't trust everyone, even if they are experienced. If someone's suggesting that you do something you don't feel comfortable doing, don't do it until you feel ready. There's no rush!

RIPS
Remember!

Getting out of a rip:

According to Surf Life Saving Australia, if you are caught in a rip:

– Don't panic – stay calm.

– Paddle parallel to the beach in the same direction as the current until you reach the breaking wave zone, then return to shore.

– If you are weak or tired of paddling, float with the current, don't fight it.

– Remember to stay calm and conserve your energy by floating on your back.

– Signal for assistance if you need help.

Sweeps

Watch out for currents which drag you along a beach. They are the result of water caught between the shore and a sand bar. Some beaches have a regular sweep – so sweet-talk the locals and hopefully they'll give you intel on how strong they are and where they usually take you. Be aware though, this may be better achieved with a six-pack of boutique ale backing up that smile and friendly enquiry. Sweeps often occur without you even realising. Their main danger is that they eventually meet up with a rip and before you know it, you're out the back in the big surf. Most surfers suggest picking a point on the shore and making sure you're always closely in line with it. Keep an eye on the rest of the surfing lineup to make sure you're not drifting.

DANGEROUS CURRENT

Tides and their impact
on surfing

Tides radically change the size of waves because they change the water depth by several metres. Tide times vary by roughly an hour every day. The amount of water moved at each tide also varies depending on the phases of the moon. Interesting isn't it? Unfortunately every surf spot has its own tide so you'll need to get the local tide chart to find out the details of low and high tides. However, there are a few rules you can use to guide you.

- **Spilling waves usually occur at high tide and plunging waves at low tide. At most beaches, the waves will increase in height as a tide rises.** *More on spilling waves later.*

- **The best time to surf is usually between high and low tides when the tide is on its way in. Waves break slower and with less white water.**

- **Faster waves are found on low tides but they are steeper and can dump faster, meaning your take-off is critical.**

Did you know: There are two high tides and two low tides in just over a 24-hour period, usually six hours apart.

For more information on tides, visit the Australian Bureau of Meteorology at www.bom.gov.au.

Understanding the
weather

Learning to read a weather map

Sounds a bit geeky, right? The stuff you snoozed through during geography class? Trust me, once you're hooked on surfing, you will love this stuff. Weather maps provide an excellent estimate of how big or small the surf will be on any given day.

Check out the map below. Those circular lines are isobars, which represent areas of equal atmospheric pressure. They also reveal the strength and direction of wind. The closer together the isobars, the stronger the wind will be. In the Southern Hemisphere, wind streams around low-pressure systems – represented with an L – in a clockwise fashion and flows anti-clockwise around high pressure systems (H). As the Australian Bureau of Meteorology explains, the space in between isobars is inversely proportional to the strength of the wind – which matters to you because the closer the lines, the stronger the winds, and the larger the waves.

Incidentally, it's no coincidence that many of the famous Californian surfers who pioneered surf breaks in Hawaii in the 1950s learned how to read weather maps. And frankly, who would dare suggest these gutsy hellmen of old were even vaguely geeky? It's old school ... and it's cool.

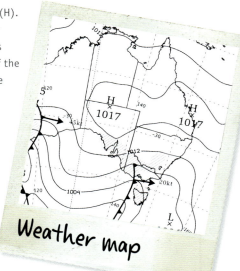

Weather map

WAM

You can also use what is called a WAM chart which specifically indicates swell size, thanks to measurement buoys and stations in the ocean that feed information to weather centres. The chart below shows the estimated size of the waves in feet as it hits the shore.

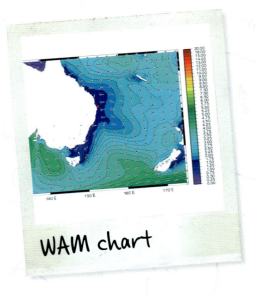

WAM chart

For more information on weather maps or to get the latest conditions, visit the Bureau of Meteorology online at www.bom.gov.au. There are plenty of surf weather sites around, but check out www.coastalwatch.com.au for the latest info and charts.

In the tropics, the rotation of the planet causes a lesser degree of friction over the earth's surface, which in turn causes the wind patterns to vary from those in locations further away from the equator. That is why tropical weather maps use streamline arrows rather than isobars to indicate wind direction!

Dayyan Neve (aka Dayyoof) has always had the talent to go all the way, but in 2005 he left Byron Bay for the breaks of Manly to put in some serious surf training which is paying off on the world stage. Mixing his surfing with yoga, swimming and gym sessions, Dayyan is passionate about making his career count Monday to Friday, but on the weekends, he surfs for himself. We caught up with him in transit as he left our shores once again in search of world-class honours.

Early days: I went for my first surf with my uncle and my cousins. It was a family trip to Wollongong and I just loved it. As soon as I got back, I got a board as quick as I could and then they couldn't stop me.

Love it: I feel so free in the ocean. I can do whatever I want. You're completely absorbed in what you're doing at that particular moment. Everything else that is happening in your life doesn't seem to matter for that moment. It's like a form of meditation. When I was young, it was all about fun, but now, it means so much more.

Career to date: I surfed on the World Qualifying Series for seven years and have been on the pro tour for two years now. I finished 32nd last year.

Learning: We're always learning in life, hey? It's that sort of sport where it doesn't matter how good you are, you are constantly learning and evolving. You're learning new things about yourself, about the ocean and about your equipment. It's constantly evolving and so are you.

Surfing Manly: The surf is always small here, well, not always, but the majority of the time it is! On the east coast the majority of swell is from the southern ocean, it's a south swell travelling up the coast from south to north so we miss the majority of it because of North Head. But hey, we work with what we have and the majority of World Champion Tour and World Qualifying Series heats are all in bad waves, so the size here works well for me.

Dayyan Neve

Beginners at Manly: The smaller Manly waves are also good for new surfers and those that are not quite there yet. The best surfers tend to go to North Steyne or Queenscliff – that leaves the area right in front of The Corso for everyone else, so we're all happy. A problem in most areas for experienced surfers is that beginners tend to get in the way and frustrate them. That's why Manly is so great because you can have your own little bit of space to express yourself and no one will get angry at you. So start right in front of The Corso and then make your way up the beach as you get better.

Dayyan Neve

Tips for beginners: Learn about the ocean, how to read it, how to play in it, what the dangers are, what the advantages are. You'll surf fine if you understand what this big mass of water is and how it behaves. Oh, and get a few lessons from someone like Matt Grainger down at Manly Surf School. He'll tell you about rips and surf conditions, all the things you need to know.

Ripped off: Make sure you don't get ripped off when buying gear. You walk into a surf shop and you don't know anything and they know that, so be a bit careful. Try and grab a friend or make friends with a surfer on the beach and get them to help you. No point buying something that looks good or is top of the range when you can't surf it and won't be able to for years!

Favourite waves: Snapper Rocks, Deadman's in Manly and Boodjidup.

Really bad waves: When the waves are just shocking I drive up the coast to Curl Curl or Whale Beach, but I'm into stand-up paddle boards as well. It's a great option for when there's no surf and great for helping with your balance.

Addicted: Surfing changes your life. It's infectious. It's like any addiction, your life ends up revolving around it.

Heroes: Richie Lovett, Benny C and Kelly Slater.

Great community: There are a bunch of great people in Manly; it's a family-oriented surfing community. Everyone loves each other, to party together and to surf together.

"I feel so free in the ocean. I can do whatever I want. You're completely absorbed in what you're doing at that particular moment."

Wipeout: Your very first wave is your very first wipeout. You fall off and pop straight back up and into it, but my first real drilling, where I was completely petrified, was at Fairy Bower. I went down for a long time and hit the rocks and cut myself up. I was only 13 and it made me really fear the ocean, but rather than deter me it just made me a little more wary of the bigger waves. But surfing is a competitive sport and at that age, you want to be better than your best friend so no, I guess it didn't really stop me at all.

Fit to SURF?

Surfing isn't just fun; this pastime will work parts of your body you didn't even know you had. Admittedly, you'll know you've got them the next day. Surfing mainly tones and strengthens. It's a great all-round workout and you won't need to fork out for membership fees to some ponced-up gym. That classic 1970s surf flick wasn't called 'Free Ride' for nothing!

Neck, the muscles along your spine, lower back, shoulders and lats work hard while paddling

Back, glutes, quads, hamstrings, shoulders, arms and pecs kick into gear when you pop up (more on that later) ...

Fingers, hands, arms, back, shoulders and lungs all work as you get through the white water

Legs and core get a workout when you catch a wave

Onshore exercises

So, surfing's a great workout. But there's also lots you can do to prepare yourself before you get in the water. Any aerobic fitness will help you at sea. A few key activities include ocean swimming, beach running, skipping, aerobics classes, cycling or spin classes at a gym, tai chi, yoga, pilates, boxing. Then there's soft sand running (not only a killer for your legs but good for quick getaways if you accidentally drop in on a heavy local), or you can try paddling a kayak, surf ski, paddleboard or canoe for upper body strength.

Many people suggest skateboarding, carveboarding or snowboarding as cross-trainers to help with balance, technique and flexibility as well as for general fitness.

Some surfers back in the 'old days' were even known to indulge in a little bullfighting, to help perfect their style, balance and bravado. Thankfully, venues for such shenanigans are thin on the ground in Oz, so you may be better off sticking to mechanical bulls in pubs during happy hour.

Balance

Balance is one of the keys to surfing. Many surfers find yoga fantastic for helping improve their balance. It also increases strength, flexibility and concentration and, super-important, it helps to prevents injury.

A quick routine of 10–15 minutes (or up to an hour if you're feeling hardcore) will have you both looking and surfing hot.

Here are some tips for a quick pre- or post-surfing session from yoga instructor Maria Kodzoman.

1. **Easy-seated pose (Sukhasana)**: Sit in an easy cross-legged position, align your knees with your hips, and flex both feet inwards towards your face. Lift your head to the sky and let your knees fall to the side. Put your hands on your knees and spend a few minutes breathing through your nose.

   Benefits: opens the hips and thigh muscles.

1. Sukhasana

2. Vrksasana

2. **Tree pose (Vrksasana):** Stand tall with your big toes touching and hands at the sternum (breastbone). Transfer your weight onto your right foot, place your left foot on your inner thigh, lift your head and focus. Hold for five breaths and alternate sides.

Benefits: balance and strength.

3. **Single leg forward bend (Parsvottanasana):** Turn your left foot outwards by around 45 degrees. Interlace your hands behind your back and stretch your arms so your fingers point to the sky. Then, pulling your abdominal muscles in towards your spine, inhale and lift your head, exhaling as you gently fold forwards towards the right knee. Hold forward for five breaths and then alternate sides.

Benefits: opens the hips and shoulder joints for increased movement.

4. **Four-limbed pose (Chaturanga Dandasana):** Begin on all fours, with your wrists in line with your shoulders, spread fingers wide. Balance on your toes, pushing into back of heels, inhale. On an exhale tuck elbows in close, lower your torso and legs to a few inches towards ground engaging stomach muscles and hold up to five breaths.

Benefits: strengthens arms, wrists and shoulders. Aids energy, faster pop-ups and boosts strength for paddling.

3. Parsvottanasana

4. Chaturanga Dandasana

Stretch adjustment sequence
(Surya Namaskar):

1. Stand tall and inhale as you raise your arms overhead.

2. As you exhale, fold your torso forward from your hips, placing your palms on the ground in front of you.

3. Inhale and lift your head to gaze up onto your fingertips.

4. Exhale. Still with your palms touching the floor, take your right leg back, and bend your left knee, stretching your heel out behind you. Gaze forward, and hold for five breaths.

5. On exhale take your left leg back to meet the right, pushing your heels back, holding your abdominal muscles in towards the spine for a flat back. Inhale.

6. Exhale. Keep your elbows in close and lower your body as if you're doing a push up – hold for five breaths.

7. Inhale, bring your legs parallel to the floor, roll onto the flats of feet with your back arched up and gaze up in a full stretch upward-dog hold for five breaths.

8. Exhale and roll onto heels, elevating your sitting bones towards the sky for downward dog. Your palms and feet should be flat on the ground.

9. Inhale, come onto the tips of your toes and gaze through your hands. Then step or jump into a full forward bend and exhale.

10. On an inhale raise your arms overhead, exhale and gaze back for mini back-bend.

11. Pull yourself back into a standing position and raise your arms above your head in a prayer position.

Reconnect with the ocean and recentre the body and breath, then alternate sides for another sequence.

Getting anised

The beginner's

Before you get started, you'll need to get your gear together. Here's what you'll need:

Board
(long and wide for stability and to keep you above the water)

Leg rope
(to help you control that big, fat board)

Board wax

Bottle of water

Sunscreen

toolkit

Outfit
(something that's practical)

Beach towel

Wettie or rashie

A dogged sense of adventure

The surfboard

Surfboards come in all shapes, sizes, colours, patterns and designs. They normally have a hand-shaped foam core which is covered with fibreglass. Machine-shaped boards are increasingly popular, cheaper and fine to use, although die-hard surfers nearly always opt for a fully personalised, hand-shaped board. It's not essential for a beginner though.

There are four main types of surfboards:

Longboard

Any board with a wide round nose that is longer than 9ft.

Mini Mal

Also with a round nose, but between 7ft and 9ft in length.

Shortboard

Any board with a pointy nose and usually under 8ft in length.

Hybrid & fun boards

A cross between a mini mal and a shortboard.

Aussies and the surfboard

When Aussie surfers witnessed a group of Californians (including future big wave hero Greg Noll) surfing on fibreglass boards at Torquay in Victoria and around Sydney in 1956, it only took seven days for boat builder Bill Clymer to create his own version. The core material, balsawood, was unavailable in Australia for another few years so local board builders ingeniously crafted hollow versions called okanuis out of plywood.

Everyone was experimenting with boards at this time, but it was the Aussies who were leading the way. Perhaps, with our pioneer spirit, we weren't afraid to test ourselves and to push the parameters of the historic sport. During the late 1960s, it was common for surfers to hack apart their boards in the garage and change the shape, the fins – anything to find a way to ride the waves better.

By 1970, boards had shrunk to less than 6 feet long and the rounded pintail was the board of choice for Aussies.

A decade later, this culture of experimentation inspired Sydney shaper Frank Williams to create a three-finned surfboard. Later refined by pro surfer and shaper Simon Anderson, the design is known today as the 'Thruster' and it remains the standard template for most progressive board design.

Even today, Aussies continue to challenge the design of the beloved surfboard, although things have come such a long way that even minimal adjustments to the 'Thruster' design are seen as revolutionary advancements. There's just not that much left to improve on, it seems!

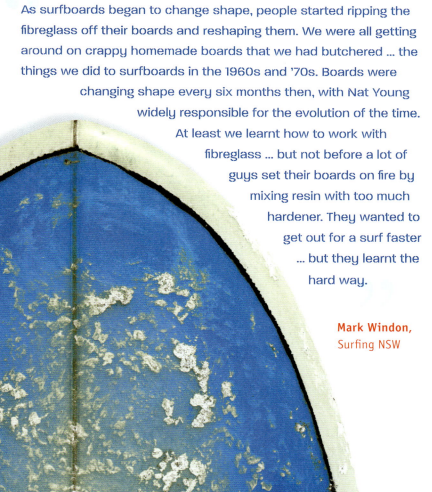

Changing shapes: a first-hand account

As surfboards began to change shape, people started ripping the fibreglass off their boards and reshaping them. We were all getting around on crappy homemade boards that we had butchered ... the things we did to surfboards in the 1960s and '70s. Boards were changing shape every six months then, with Nat Young widely responsible for the evolution of the time. At least we learnt how to work with fibreglass ... but not before a lot of guys set their boards on fire by mixing resin with too much hardener. They wanted to get out for a surf faster ... but they learnt the hard way.

Mark Windon,
Surfing NSW

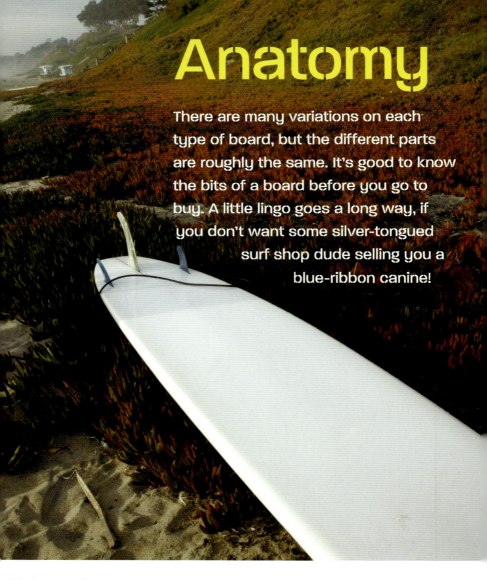

Anatomy

There are many variations on each type of board, but the different parts are roughly the same. It's good to know the bits of a board before you go to buy. A little lingo goes a long way, if you don't want some silver-tongued surf shop dude selling you a blue-ribbon canine!

# of a surfboard

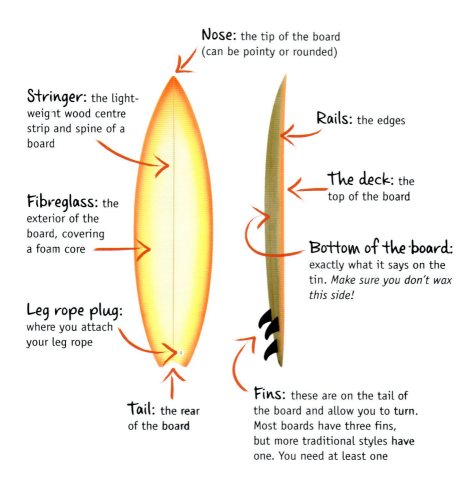

Nose: the tip of the board (can be pointy or rounded)

Stringer: the lightweight wood centre strip and spine of a board

Rails: the edges

The deck: the top of the board

Fibreglass: the exterior of the board, covering a foam core

Bottom of the board: exactly what it says on the tin. *Make sure you don't wax this side!*

Leg rope plug: where you attach your leg rope

Tail: the rear of the board

Fins: these are on the tail of the board and allow you to turn. Most boards have three fins, but more traditional styles have one. You need at least one

Tail options

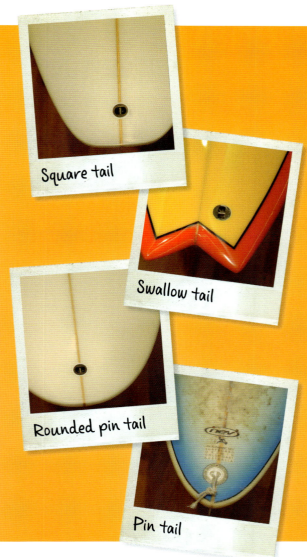

Square tail

Swallow tail

Rounded pin tail

Pin tail

There are four main types of tail: square tail, swallow tail, rounded pin and pin. While you won't need to know this right now, you will in time. As a beginner, stick to a rounded pin or square tail.

Square tail and swallow tail: These both allow you to turn abruptly and are usually used on shortboards.

Rounded pin tail and pin tail: Rounded pins provide a smoother turn. Pin tails are used in big-wave riding or on super long boards to allow better hold and speed. You don't want to spin out, watching key moments of your soon-to-be-ended life flash before your eyes as you careen down the face of a big one ... do you?

A quick chat ...

with BEN MACARTNEY, surf forecaster with Coastalwatch

Coastalwatch: We have more than 100 cameras across Australia and some in Hawaii. From those we put together surf reports and forecasts so people like you and I can go online and check out stats on everything from swell size to wind direction. This means that surfers can make more informed choices about where to go surfing.

For beginners: The idea is to help novices, and people with only a bit of experience, get the information to help them make sensible surf choices. We all want to know when and where to surf. You can't teach common sense, but we try and make sure people at least know what to expect and which areas are and aren't suitable for them.

Surf forecasting: Accuracy is the key. We try our best to get it right and often we are forecasting four to seven days out and working out how the weather will impact on the surf.

> "The idea is to help novices, and people with only a bit of experience, get the information to help them make sensible surf choices."

First wave: I was really young and took turns with my little brother at riding on our dad's back at North Bondi in Sydney.

Love surfing: I love everything about it ... the sense of freedom you get from being in harmony with nature and the ocean.

Favourite break: Definitely G-land (Bay of Grajagan, Indonesia) and in Australia, it would have to be Tamarama.

Message for beginner surfers: Be persistent and hang in there. It may suck when you are learning but the day will come when you are rewarded for all your effort. On the other hand, not everyone is blessed with natural ability.

The ocean: Clichéd but true, treat this baby with respect, just how you would like to be treated.

Best piece of advice you've been given: Hold onto your board.

Surfing heroes? My dad, he taught me and is still surfing today, probably even more than me.

Where do I fit?

A beginner surfer

You're known as a 'kook' if you have only been surfing for a year or two. During this time, most people are still trying to master paddling, wave riding and duck diving. Just making it back to your car in one piece is a challenge conquered at this stage. The easy swagger and too-cool-for-school nonchalance of the true surfer is a way off yet.

An intermediate surfer

You're an average Joe if you've been surfing for a few years, can paddle confidently and have a solid understanding of the ocean, specifically rips and currents. You can confidently surf on your own, ride waves successfully and can control your board, getting out of the way of other surfers.

An experienced surfer

If you qualify for this category, we salute you! You're an experienced surfer after you've been on the waves for many years, have a fantastic understanding of the ocean and surf conditions, can paddle for long periods, have excellent control of your board and regularly undertake tricks and turns on waves. Not to mention having the requisite cred to confidently recount tales of epic surf safaris and scoring all-time waves, be they partially fraudulent or otherwise.

Longboards are recommended for beginners because they're big, slow and steady. They sit like cruise ships in the ocean, nice and stable, are thicker than shortboards, and have rounded corners. It's no coincidence Hawaiian surfers call them tankers.

Initially, you should avoid small, thin trendy models or the pointy nose shortboard – they are just too hard to stand up and stay on! They require greater balance and control, and don't float or paddle as well. You also don't want to spend all your time falling off ... just some of the time will be enough.

Get a board that's about your height – plus the length of your arm stretched above your head. A board taller than your reach is fine but the longer and heavier it is, the harder it will be to carry and transport. (Don't forget to make sure you can carry it and fit it onto your car!) Make sure the board is big and thick enough so you can easily sit and float on it in the ocean. If it sinks while you are sitting on it, take it back.

BUYING TIPS: Most surf shops let you rent boards so you can try before you buy. Find a shop with plenty of choice. If nothing seems right, don't rush the purchase. Go to the next shop until you find what feels and looks right to you. Take a seasoned surfer or really drill the shop assistant to ensure it's the right board for you. If they realise you're determined and set on the ol' twenty questions, they'll probably drop all pretence of hustling and fix you up with the real deal so they can get back to their surf mags more quickly!

Rather than metric measurement, surfboards across the globe are sold in feet and inches. It's partly a throwback to the shared ancestry between boats and boards and also because the US, the biggest market for surfboards, uses imperial measurements.

Which board for me?

Hard or soft boards?

Boards come in both hard (fibreglass) and soft varieties. You can learn on either. If you're serious about surfing, seasoned surfers tend to suggest you start with a hard board, because you're forced to learn on the kind of board you will surf with forever. However, most admit that the new, more advanced soft boards (the originals rode slightly worse than soggy mattresses!) really do help beginners, a bit like training wheels on a bike. These pros and cons will help you make up your own mind ...

HARD BOARDS (fibreglass)

Pros:

- Look amazing
- Are the real deal
- You won't have to upgrade quickly, and
- Allow you to learn on the equipment you will use forever.

Cons:

- More expensive ($400–$2000 for bottom of the range styles)
- Much harder to learn on
- Less forgiving and you'll get knocked around (expect bruises and more)
- There's more diversity which means confusion for a beginner, and
- Waxing required.

SOFT BOARDS

Pros:

- Designed for beginners with stability in mind
- They float well
- Don't hurt so much when you get smashed by them
- Have rounded fins that don't cut
- Are reasonably lightweight
- No waxing required
- Safe, and
- Cheap ($100–$400).

Cons:

- Surfing is meant to be cool, right? These are not necessarily!
- Allow you to create lazy 'soft board' habits (such as not needing to control your board as much because you're less likely to mangle yourself with it)
- Can snap in half when you start to get adventurous (I can vouch for that!)
- Need to upgrade once you really get the hang of it
- Might be hard to on-sell, and
- Cause rashes more easily.

Waxing boards

Wax is the stuff that helps your feet grip the board. You don't wax soft boards because the foam itself grips well, but you do need to wax hard boards. Here are some tips:

- Wax the top only, applying sideways first and then back and forth in lines rather than circles.

- Wax all the way to the end of the board (where the fins are). There is no need to go right to the front on shortboards. On longboards, though, it is essential if you want to pull off the ultimate cool longboard move, hanging ten: the art within the art. Focus on a large area where your feet will go.

- Put a heavy coat on when you're learning, so the wax beads.

- Some boards have traction pads stuck to them – you don't need to wax these.

- After a few surfs, you can break up the wax with a wax comb (bought from surf shops), a stick, a stone or a shell to help create further traction. Even grandad's old comb will do the trick if you're on a budget.

- There are four general types of wax, which relate to water temperatures (cold, cool, warm and tropical).

Waxing — too much is never enough

I meticulously waxed my hard board for the first time ... or I thought I was being meticulous, until I got it down to the beach for a photoshoot for this book and was nearly laughed off the beach by the boys. It seems you can never have enough wax (probably a good rule all round when hitting the beach!). I was quickly told they all wax their boards before every surf and they wondered how I'd managed to stay on my board at all with just one poor attempt – well done to me I say!

Don't wax inside

Okay, note to self – don't be a princess! When I got my hard board, I proudly took it inside for my first ever wax. I laid it out on the living room floor and set to work. When I thought I had finished (I hadn't – remember, too much wax is never enough!) I tried in vain to get it back into the board bag. Having difficulty at floor level I hoisted the board upright only to encounter my worst surfing accident to date (the black eyes and bluebottles I had experienced in the water were nothing compared to this!). Forgetting that a board is long and living rooms have lights, I hit a very old, very thick glass lightshade which, I am not kidding, dropped in shards like little knives all over me and my new board bag. I collapsed to the floor and came to in a pool of blood. I literally had little knife slices all over my face, shoulders and feet and all over my board bag – nice!

Lesson — wax in the open air away from sharp objects!

Maintaining
your board

These tips are especially important for hard boards, because they are the ones to suffer the worst from bumps and falls. The old softie is in fact, pretty hardy and can take a bit of a beating.

- Invest in a board bag or board sock (which is exactly what it suggests!).

- Get some roof racks if your car allows (portable soft racks are very good as well, are excellent value and can be found in most surf shops). Chucking boards into cars can cause damage over time. Plus removing molten wax off the seats and carpet is a Herculean task best avoided.

- Hose it down after each surf.

- Try not to hit walls, trees, other surfboards, any bigger surfers than you, or anything really, to avoid dents or, worse, internal breaks.

- Keep it out of the sun when you're not surfing because UV can cause the lamination (the outer fibreglass shell) to break and it also melts your wax!

- Fix dents with a ding repair kit – or take it to a professional – to stop any water leaking into the core and especially the timber stringer. If you let too much water soak into the wood the board will soon be irreparable.

- If you are riding a shortboard (you'll get there!), make sure you cover the nose with a rubber guard to stop it from hurting you or anyone else. It'll also help guard it from damage.

Board repair kit

If you do buy a fibreglass board, then it pays to grab a board repair kit. They usually include a polyester resin, a hardener and a fibreglass mat (oh, and instructions). You should apply these when you get any dings in your board to stop any leakage into the foam core.

Repairing your board is actually a rite of passage that everyone should attempt at least once. Just be careful to mix the combustible chemicals correctly or you will have what's called a hot mix and may be tearily calling the fire department within minutes.

Leg ropes

Leg ropes are urethane cords that strap to your back leg with a velcro patch to help you control your board. Not all surfers use these (especially old school longboarders), but they are helpful for beginners. They help stop you from losing your board and help prevent your board from hitting someone nearby (you can't always prevent that ... but best to try). There are also quick-release leg ropes, which attach to your calf rather than your ankle and allow you to press a lever to release you from the board if you become stuck or snagged. Either way, grab a relatively long one, and make sure you hold onto it when walking into the waves (tripping on your leg rope is not the best look!).

Danny Wills

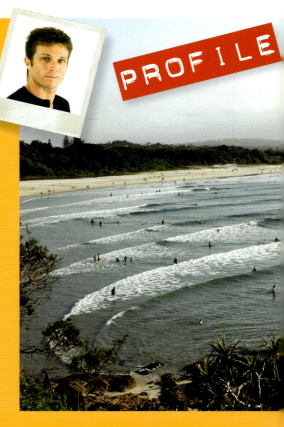

Byron Bay lad Danny Wills has been mixing it with the world's best for 20 years, once stealing a heat from Kelly Slater. The natural footer, who never leaves home with less than six boards in his bag, reached third in the World Qualifying Series in 2000, but despite surfing waves across the globe, says The Pass and The Wreck in Byron will always be his favourite spots. He loves barrels and round-horse cutbacks and, fresh from competition in Tahiti, we chatted to him about life on the road and traversing a generally crowded Pass break.

"There are heaps of collisions at The Pass; it's absolutely crazy. All the time I have boards going over my head. It's nuts ..."

Early days: I had four sisters and we just hung at the beach. Having five kids, it's like ... what do you do with them? But for some reason I liked it. Apparently I wanted to surf all day and never wanted to leave. It was just in me. There's a photo of me and I'm about two and a half riding my own board at The Pass. I actually started surfing when I was 18 months old. My dad used to put me on the nose of his mal and put some floaties on me and we'd surf together. But then I got my own board and surfed the whitewash until I was about five. Then I could catch waves and surf the face of the wave and it was like 'see you later'. The Pass wasn't crowded back then so it was okay.

Inspiration: My dad was a huge inspiration for my surfing. He started when he was 10 and he's still surfing now at 55.

Advice for beginners:

1. Get the right teacher with the right temperament. You'll learn quicker that way.

2. Avoid the lineup until you're ready. I'm all for people learning to surf, it's unreal, but don't get out there in everyone's way until you have the gist of it and you're doing okay. At The Pass there are people who get really close to surfers like myself but they have no ability and it can get really dangerous.

Collisions: There are heaps of collisions at The Pass; it's absolutely crazy. All the time I have boards going over my head. It's nuts, hey. You're dodging, trying to get out of the way, slowing up on waves, pulling back. It's due to people not knowing where they should be. I say, just hang back a bit and enjoy the smaller waves; you'll have more fun that way and get more waves and you'll be out of people's way.

Danny Wills

Favourite wave: The Pass, I love it, it's amazing. It's just started to get really good this year. It comes and goes. Two years ago we had an amazing run where it broke for three months straight. It's definitely not the best wave in the world, but it's the best fun for me. It's that thing of growing up here and I'll surf it a couple of times a day if it's breaking. It's good when it gets bigger too because it gives the more experienced surfers a chance to have a good go at it. I also like Lennox Head. I went there when I was nine and I still remember it.

Locals only at The Pass: Yeah, there was a bit of tribalism back in the day. Me and my mates gave the 'locals only' sign a re-spray once. We got there early in the morning and gave it a touch up.

Competition: Surfing is a different sport in that respect – surfing for yourself and having to compete. You have to be selfish. One minute you're in a motel room talking with your mates and the next minute you're out there trying to beat them.

Hard to explain: If there is stuff going on in my life and I'm troubled or stressed then you just head out and it washes away. It's hard to explain it to people who don't surf. It's like anyone who plays sport I guess, you go out there and hit a tennis ball around and it just clears your mind.

Hanging with the kids: I'm looking forward to being able to be hands-on with my kids more and watching them grow. I'll compete this year and see how I feel. I've been travelling for 20 years and it works out to be about nine months away pretty solidly. The last eight years we've taken the kids the majority of the way, but it's harder now they're older, because they are starting to miss a bit of school. We're all sort of feeling it so to let go of it, while sad, hey, it will be good too.

Heroes: Definitely Kelly Slater and Tom Carroll. Kelly, for being the most professional and the best, I think, that's ever been and Tom, purely for being the most aggressive, powerful surfer out there and he's sort of my size so that is always pushing me. I was in a movie with Tom Carroll when I was 12 (*All Down the Line*) so he has been a hero ever since.

Best advice ever given: It's not necessarily what people say, hey, it's often the timing. I remember in my first year on the tour I was really struggling and I hadn't been through a heat in 10 contests and that's pretty bad. I was questioning myself and Luke Egan took me aside and said, 'Look, you're good enough, you just have to believe in yourself'. I can't remember his exact words but the next thing I knew, I was through a heat and then I drew Kelly Slater and beat him.

What to wear

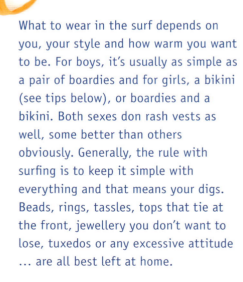

What to wear in the surf depends on you, your style and how warm you want to be. For boys, it's usually as simple as a pair of boardies and for girls, a bikini (see tips below), or boardies and a bikini. Both sexes don rash vests as well, some better than others obviously. Generally, the rule with surfing is to keep it simple with everything and that means your digs. Beads, rings, tassles, tops that tie at the front, jewellery you don't want to lose, tuxedos or any excessive attitude … are all best left at home.

Boardies

Boardies look and feel great. Make sure they fit snugly, especially around the waist, otherwise they'll move around in the water, and even ... fall off. There are male and female versions and they come in short, medium and long lengths. Medium is a good option if you don't already have a preference.

It happens to us all ...

> I lost my boardies once, it happens to everyone at some point. You crash from a wave and it all sort of comes undone. I just floated around for a bit until I found them and shoved them back on before anyone even noticed. It was pretty funny.

Perth Standlick of Bondi Beach, 18, rode his first wave at the age of seven. He was an impressive grom and is expected to grace the world tour some time in the near future.

Bikinis look and feel great but they can also come off in the surf. If you are going to wear a bikini, here are a few tips:

- Make sure it's tight fitting (it will loosen in the water).
- Halter neck and sports-style tops will hold you in best.
- Tie and double-tie knots and bows, and make sure they are tight.
- Keep an eye on things while out there!
- If it comes off, gracefully go underwater and fix it. If it's during a wipeout, vanity comes after safety. Besides, the wipeout has already stripped you of your dignity.

The quick beach change for gals

- Grab a big beach towel and wrap it around your waist
- If you have a car door, open the door and stand behind it for extra privacy
- Chuck your bikini bottom or boardies on under the towel, and
- Put your bikini on under your T-shirt with a bit of creativity.

And you're done! The quicker the better. No one will even notice.

Bikinis

Rash vests

As the name suggests, these nylon and lyrca tops stop a rash developing on your torso from your board. This can be one of the worst things about surfing and can sometimes develop into nasty sea ulcers, so it's best to be prepared. Rashies are also handy for girls to help prevent your bikini top heading south ... if you get the drift. They come in long and short sleeves and in tank top styles and some also have UV protection.

Long sleeve

Short sleeve

Tank top

T-shirts

T-shirts were okay in the old days, as were silent movies, horses and buggies, and dental work pre-anesthetic ... but most surfers find them uncomfortable and icky when wet. Try a rash vest instead.

Other accessories

Various other items that can come in handy, although not necessary for beginners, include booties, helmets, and gloves.

Wetsuits

You might also want to wear a wetsuit in cooler weather, depending on the time of year. Here's the lowdown on wetsuits.

Wetsuits explained

Wetsuits are made from a stretchy rubber material, and are designed to keep you warm in cold water temperatures. They do this by allowing a small amount of water into the suit which is warmed by your body temperature before it's trapped between you and the suit, forming your very own insulation. They also protect you from the sun and keep the wind out, not to mention shielding you from nasties like jellyfish, lice or the occasional garbage – human and other – that drifts into the lineup.

Sydney water temperatures range from 15 to 25 degrees so in the cooler months, on windy days, or if you're planning to stay out for hours and prefer not to get hypothermia, you might consider a wetsuit. You can buy suits to cope for arctic conditions, but seeing we have plenty of sun, something around 3/2 mm should be fine. This measurement describes the thickness of the suit (the first number is the torso, the second number denotes thickness of the arms and legs).

These days, wetsuits are lightweight, flexible and pretty comfortable. Buy a full suit (known as a steamer), a half piece (known as a spring suit), a half piece without arms (known as a short john), a wetsuit top (a vest) or wetsuit shorts – it's up to you.

For specific water temperatures for any location, visit www.bom.gov.au

Also know as a 'steamer'

A 'spring suit'

Full suit

Half suit

Half piece

Top & shorts

Known as a
'short john'

A 'wetsuit vest & shorts'

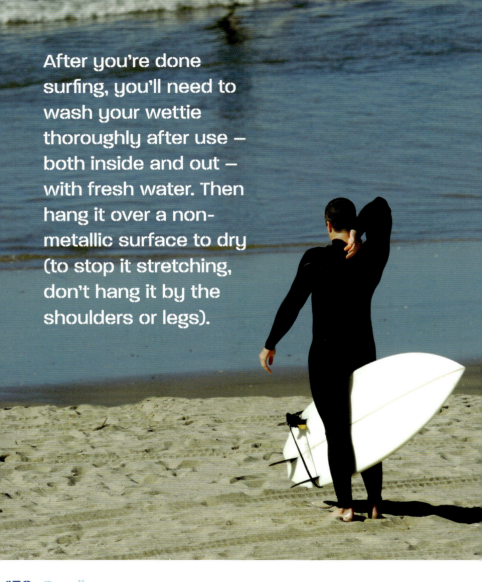

After you're done surfing, you'll need to wash your wettie thoroughly after use – both inside and out – with fresh water. Then hang it over a non-metallic surface to dry (to stop it stretching, don't hang it by the shoulders or legs).

Choosing a wetsuit

When you're ready to buy a wetsuit, there are a few things to remember:

- Make sure it's snug, not so tight that you can't breathe or move your shoulders comfortably, but tight enough that it's an effort getting it on. If it's too big, the water won't trap, the suit won't work and you may be mistaken for the Michelin Man's stunt double.

- Buy for comfort not style or whichever groovy surf star is featured in the full colour brochure.

- Make sure the seams are smooth, so they won't aggravate or rub your skin.

- Suits with key pockets are great and will put a few carpark vandals out of business.

- Suits are made for men and women – make sure you get the right one. It really will fit better!

- Straight from the shelf is fine!

Wetsuit tips

The first few times you're heading out for a surf with your new wetsuit, you could try getting your suit on at home before you hit the beach. They're tricky to put on until you've had a bit of practise. Scrunch up the legs and pull them up over your body, then the arms and then use the long cord to zip it shut. But admittedly, driving in rubber on a stinkin' Aussie summer day is less than fun.

Do I need lessons?

Even if you're a strong swimmer or have tried other water sports, it pays to get some help, even if it's just one lesson. Surf schools have popped up all over the world. There are plenty in Australia and Bondi that you can visit to learn a few basic techniques.

Reading this book or any other surf book is excellent as it will teach you about the ocean and show you the tools you need, but the essential next step is to have someone watch you and critique you on what you are doing right and wrong. I took three lessons and then hit the water on my own. I actually went back for more advanced lessons after a few months to help take me to the next level.

If you can, book yourself into a surf school for a lesson or two, or even a surf camp if you have a spare weekend or few days. It will do wonders for your confidence and your surfing.

Barton Lynch

Talking with former world champ Barton Lynch, it's hard to see how such a relaxed individual had the competitive drive to make it all the way to the top and stay there for some time. This incredibly cool character started surfing the beach breaks as a kid, developing a flexible style with flawless, fluid routines that eventually saw him reach world champ status in 1988 thanks to an amazing display at Hawaii's famed Pipeline. He spent 13 consecutive years in the top 16, and enjoyed 17 World Championship Tour victories before retiring in March 1998. A great friend of the Learn to Surf series, we caught up with Barton on the back porch of his Avalon home to chew the fat about his years in the surf world.

Early on: I spent my first 11 years at Whale Beach, then eight years in Mosman, 10 years at Manly and now I'm back at Whale Beach where I've lived for the last 15 years.

Home is always the best: Everywhere has its day and I just like to be on the spot on the day regardless of where it is. I love to surf at my home spot of Whale Beach. I love riding waves that tube and I love being towed into them by jet skis. Actually, I love everything about surfing really.

NSW: Pretty much the whole coastline is littered with waves. At the south end of the coast there are more reef breaks and up north there are more point breaks. I love the Forster area in the north and the Ulladulla area in the south and there's nothing better than Sydney in a big swell.

Crowds: Being able to get information about conditions from a web page is a bummer because traditionally surfers developed a sense of where was good to go and where not to go, and the better surfers enjoyed the better waves. Now although technology is good for many reasons, it has added to the crowds and has had an impact on the number of waves people can catch. As surfers we are selfish little buggers … it's always better if there are less people out there.

Inspiration: My boards definitely give me moments of inspiration. I probably own 40 boards right now and it's still not enough. With the advancement of surfboard technology, there is now a board for every weather and wave condition. And then there's getting in the car with your mates, hitting the roads, searching for waves and hoping you are going to score. I love that about surfing.

Thinking ahead: I don't really look back on old surfing road trips. I like planning ahead. I am always planning where I am going next – which right now is Hawaii.

Barton Lynch

Balance: How to balance surfing with other commitments? Shit, if anyone knows the answer to that, let me know. Use the flat and shitty days when the waves aren't good to work and get your commitments out of the way so when it's going off, you can blow off work and go for a surf. And the same goes for partying too. There is no worse feeling than missing some really good surf 'cause you're hung over.

Sponsored surfing: Anywhere money is involved, things get complicated. It takes a lot of commitment and dedication to surf for a living and it's great that people are able to do that. There is limited opportunity in surfing and particularly for Aussie surfers – the marketplace isn't big enough to support the amount of talent we have. There has been a complete commercial exploitation of the surf culture over the past 20 years but the simple joy of riding a wave has never changed.

World title: As a young kid, all I dreamt about was surfing and winning the world title. It was always my goal, so having achieved that means that sleep has come easily ever since. I've been lucky enough to have lived my dreams to date. The year before I won, in 1987, I was in the lead at the halfway mark and thought the world title was mine, but I collapsed under the pressure of leading. The final event of the year was at Manly and I thought I was going to win in front of my mum and family at home. So at the start of 1988, I felt like I had missed my destiny. I was heartbroken really so I was dwelling on what I had missed rather than what was ahead. As it turned out in the final event in 1988, five people were in contention for the title and everything went my way so at the end of the day, I was the world champion. Every surfer dreams of winning in Hawaii and at Pipeline. It's the most challenging wave in the world to surf and to win there has a lot more prestige and a lot more personal satisfaction so even though I felt I missed my destiny in 1987, I received something so much better in 1988.

Surfing heroes: Wayne Lynch, one of the great goofy footers in the sport and he happened to have the same name as me so it was a natural fit. Terry Richardson and all the great legends of the sport, Mark Richards, Midget Farrelly, and the great Hawaiian surfer Larry Bertlemann. These days, I think my heroes are more in the moment, it's more about what you see going on around you. Perhaps my mum is my hero.

3.

Surf theory: The stuff you need to know

Paddling

When most people think of surfing, they imagine riding waves, the feeling of freedom and the odd wipeout. I'm not sure many beginners actually think about the paddling, but to be honest, it's one of the most important parts of surfing – and one of the most tiring. You will spend more time paddling out and around than you will actually catching waves.

How to paddle:

- Wait for the waves to lull before you head out, to conserve energy.
- Paddle as if you were swimming freestyle, with one hand in the water at a time.
- One arm should be pulling water back as the other is stretching ahead to start the motion again.
- Use long, deep, even strokes for greater power and speed.
- Keep your elbows bent and cup your hands to ensure you push water back with every stroke. Some surfers even use webbed gloves.
- The nose of the board should be just clearing the surface.
- Keep your feet almost together. This will make the board a little less stable but helps reduce drag.
- Lift your head, which helps your strokes ... and also helps you see where you are going!

Paddling tips:

- One for the girls: arch your back instead of putting your chest flat on the board to save your boobs from unnecessary pain! It will get easier as your back muscles strengthen.
- Finding it hard to paddle? You might be lying too far back on the board and there's too much water to push. Or maybe you're too far forward, water is lapping over the deck, and you're risking nose diving ...
- Avoid paddling – jump from the rocks into deeper water. This is an option only for more experienced surfers. It's great because you go straight out near the lineup but it's dangerous and scary for inexperienced surfers and swimmers. More on this later.

too far back

too far forward

just right!

The best place to learn to paddle is in wave-free water so go out on a flat day to brush up on your skills. Some of the greatest watermen in surfing history were keen long distance paddlers, utilising special paddle boards, in both ocean and flat water racing.

Your feet –
goofy or natural?

In surfing, snowboarding and skateboarding, you're either a natural footer or a goofy footer, which relates to which foot you put at the front when you pop up or stand up to ride a wave. It's the same concept as being right- or left-handed. So which one are you?

Lie on your stomach on the ground or on your board and, pushing with your arms, do the pop up motion. Whichever foot you instinctively place forward will be the foot you'll use every time. If you were a little unsure, try both feet and see which feels the most comfortable.

Still unsure? Try this activity. Stand up straight with your feet together. Slowly fall forwards while keeping your feet together and just before you fall, you'll move your feet to stop yourself. Your dominant foot will always go forward. Think of how you would naturally defend yourself, kind of like a boxer stands, and that is usually the stance you will adopt when surfing.

Jumping from the rocks

Hmmm ... you know how I said I was nearly killed on my third surf? Slight exaggeration, but my friend did mention that the surf was too big and would take us way too long to get out the back, so suggested we jump in from North Bondi rocks. Well, I'm usually up for anything, so off we went. It wasn't till I was standing out there and the waves were literally crashing straight onto me and the rocks that I had second thoughts ... let's see – big waves, breaking onto rocks, me on my softie, only my third surf, no idea how to jump, let alone much else about surfing. The plan sounded simple: jump, end up out the back, and head back to shore to battle it out the normal way. Well, I did it, but I have to admit my heart was in my throat the whole time.

Although we beginners LOVE the accomplished surfers, I think sometimes they forget what it was like to be a beginner and what we are capable of. Baby steps, people! Nice for them to have confidence in us ... but too much confidence and it could end in disaster!

Tackling the white water

Most beginner surfers will testify that getting past the white water is a bit of an effort. Sometimes even the smallest waves can catch you off guard, knocking you off your feet. But as a newcomer to the sport, you'll spend a lot of your time getting bounced around in this beloved white wash so a few techniques to assist are like gold. First, always make sure the board is pointed towards the wave, never parallel to the beach and between you and the wave, like I did on my first day. Yes, the force of the wave will ensure your board has a spectacular ride through the air before it lands and hits you in the face.

There are a few options to get through white water. They include ...

1. Pushing over the

... the closer you are to the breaking wave, the stronger the white water will be ...

wave

As you approach the wave, point the board directly into the wave, but push down slightly on the tail of the board so it lifts the nose and the white water can go under you more easily. You need to get a firm grip on the board and once you're over, get straight back into paddling mode to gain forward movement again! A great technique for small white water waves.

2. Duck dives

A more sophisticated way of cutting through waves by plunging yourself down and underneath the wave while it passes. When you approach the wave, grab the rails and push down on the nose of the board, plunging yourself and the board underwater. Plant one knee on the deck of the board, pushing down as hard as you can with your hands on the rails. Allow your free leg to kick out to thrust you forward.

The aim is to dive as deep as you can before the wave reaches you. As the wave begins to pass, put the board out in front of you, and then surface, hopefully past the wave! If not, it can be a little messy, but you'll soon learn the art of timing.

Duck dives are only possible with shortboards. Be careful to push down heavily in the first instance to avoid the wave catching the board and pushing it back into your face with the usual consequence – acute embarrassment and a bloody nose for either you or the poor bugger caught too close to your mess-up.

3. Eskimo rolls

A common and easy way to beat waves by rolling over and letting the water pass over the board, especially useful for bigger boards. When you approach the wave, simply grab the rails (side of the board), lift your upper body, put your weight on one side and roll yourself over in similar fashion to a kayak Eskimo roll. Head under the wave, keeping the nose from catching it, and sink down underneath it. Once it passes, roll over and get going again! Eskimo rolls are possible with longboards and shortboards.

Some days the white water can get you down. You just can't seem to get out there and you're close to giving up. Remember that every surfer faces this regularly. Either push through it or simply surf the white water today and try another day. There's no shame in that. The greater shame would be giving up so early in the game.

Hanging out on your board

If you go out past the white water to the open swell, it's a beautiful thing — quiet, peaceful and scenic. The best thing to do is sit on your board and take it in while you wait for a wave. You do this by pushing down on the rails gently, popping your legs on either side of the board and sliding your body up the board to the middle. Watch that the board doesn't take off on its own from under you. Keep a firm grip on the rails and move slowly. Sit with a straight back watching the waves and the beautiful surroundings.

Turning your board around

Turning your board around is
paramount to catching waves.
When waiting, you will face out to
sea, but to catch them, you'll need to turn
the board 180 degrees for your departure. The
quicker you can turn, the more waves you will catch.
Turning while lying on your board is slow and cumbersome.
Most surfers turn while in a seated position. The further you slide
your bum back on your board, the easier it is. Do little circles with
your feet and lower legs to help with movement in the water. Practise
perfecting your turns when the waves are quiet as you'll only have a
few seconds when that set arrives.

Somewhere under here your legs are doing little circles to help you move!

Stephanie Gilmore

Stephanie Gilmore is being watched by surfers the world over after her quick rise to victory on the women's tour to take out the ASP Women's World Title in 2007. Many believe she will be the next Beachley and will dominate the sport for years to come with her advanced style and gorgeous personality.

The beginning:

My dad gave me a bodyboard when I was 10 and that's how it started!

Surfing loves:

The ocean is such a refreshing place. Surfing is more of a lifestyle and it allows you to spend a lot of time out there dreaming. I've been in the ocean all my life and I love it.

Youthful aspirations: I played a lot of sports, lots of grass hockey, soccer and athletics, everything I could. I actually wanted to go to the Olympics and thought I would become a professional runner.

Best surfing moment: There have been so many but winning the world title was definitely a key moment. Getting better and better is a highlight but there are many special moments along the way.

Home break: Snapper Rocks, Tweed Heads.

Injuries: I've been very fortunate and haven't had any really bad injuries. I'm hoping it will stay this way for the majority of my career.

Advice for beginners: Realise there is another side to the ocean and that you have to be patient and can't control it. On the other hand, you have to make sure you have fun no matter what you are doing and realise that the ocean is there to enjoy.

Women's surfing: There are a lot of younger girls out there surfing now which is great. There are a lot of girls out there showing guys that they can surf too and that surfing is something that is a general thing to be enjoyed by everyone. I think pretty soon, surfing will be truly equal for sure.

Sharks: I have never seen a shark in the water. Well, I don't really know, I hope I haven't. You can see dolphins and get them most days, so I guess there could have been a shark at some point. I hope not.

Important message: We have to make sure that we are looking after the ocean and that we are preserving it otherwise it will be gone. The ocean, nature generally, is really gorgeous and we have to keep educating people and creating awareness in the new generation that they need to care for the ocean. We need to be careful about what footprints we are leaving behind in the sand.

A bit about waves

All waves are different but they can be loosely divided into two categories:

1. **Spilling (or rolling or crumbling) waves:** This is when waves crumble on themselves and offer a slow build-up of white wash. They form where there's a gradual slope on the sea floor. They break slowly with little power and are perfect for beginners. They are gentle. So embrace them.

2. **Plunging (or dumping) waves:** This is where the wave breaks from the top to the bottom and sometimes creates a tunnel which surfers can ride in and along. They form when water gets shallow quickly. They're powerful and usually ridden by experienced surfers ... and, unfortunately, occasionally by those who really should know better. The danger is that because they generally break in shallow water they can cause you to nose dive into the sand, a common cause of spinal injury.

Types of
wave breaks

There are three main wave breaks:

1. Beach break: As the name suggests, a beach break occurs when waves break over sand. They change size and shape because the sand beneath them is constantly shifting thanks to currents, waves, tides and moving sandbanks. These are the wave breaks you're most likely to encounter, so choose wisely and savour.

2. Reef or rock shelf break: Powerful and heavy plunging waves form when water from the deep sea moves in over shallow reefs, rocks or man-made structures. Often resulting in the picturesque tubular wave, experienced surfers have been known to foam at the mouth, sign away their first-born or experience religious epiphany over reef breaks. But the chance of injury is greatly increased for beginners attempting to surf these locations, so take heed and keep your eyes open at all times.

3. Point break: This is when waves break around a headland or rocky point. They usually break in a single direction, left or right, which is determined by the headland itself. Waves are usually longer and peel, making for a great ride for all experience levels. You can usually jump in from the rocks and avoid the white water as well, but make sure the waves are not too large. You're a beginner remember!

Beach break

Reef break

Point break

Peak

Back

Tube

Face

The parts of a
wave

Waves are usually measured from the trough to the peak, but after you've been around the shores for a bit, you'll hear surfers refer to them in this way ... knee-high, waist-high, chest-high, head-high, overhead etc.

More specifically, there has been an ongoing debate among surfers about how waves are measured, with Hawaiians tending to underestimate wave height by measuring from behind. No matter what, every surfer will be guilty of exaggerating the size of a ride they felt was exceptional at some stage in their surfing life.

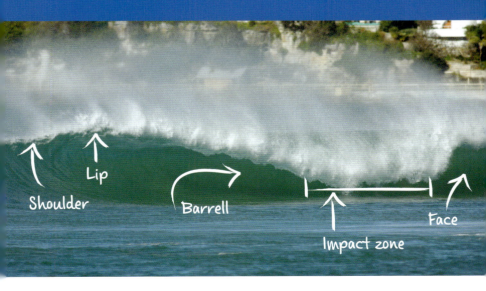

Shoulder

Lip

Barrell

Impact zone

Face

Waves for **beginners**

You should start surfing in waves that are waist-height or less. They should also be crumbling (or spilling) rather than curling over like those amazing waves you see in surf magazines. Your waves are more like a small mess of water that has enough power to push you in. Avoid ones that smash you with a thud or you might find yourself pining for other, gentler sports such as skydiving, Formula 1, cage fighting and running with the bulls.

Look for where the line of surfers is; they're usually out a fair way and sitting on their boards. Under no circumstances should you paddle out there (even if a more experienced friend tries to drag you out). The white water, the waves breaking in close to shore, is where you want to stay for quite a while.

Try to find a less crowded spot where other beginners are congregating, and then paddle out.

If you really want to surf but the waves are just too big – don't do it. Go for a swim in between the flags instead or watch and learn from experienced surfers. Your pride, your board and your yet-to-be-born grandchildren will thank you.

Catching your
first wave

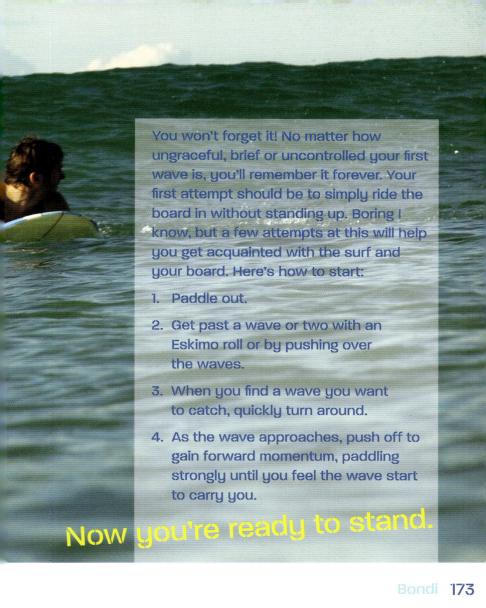

You won't forget it! No matter how ungraceful, brief or uncontrolled your first wave is, you'll remember it forever. Your first attempt should be to simply ride the board in without standing up. Boring I know, but a few attempts at this will help you get acquainted with the surf and your board. Here's how to start:

1. Paddle out.

2. Get past a wave or two with an Eskimo roll or by pushing over the waves.

3. When you find a wave you want to catch, quickly turn around.

4. As the wave approaches, push off to gain forward momentum, paddling strongly until you feel the wave start to carry you.

Now you're ready to stand.

Rusty Miller

FORMER US CHAMPION AND BYRON BAY LOCAL

Byron Bay is home to legendary surfer Rusty Miller, the US champion of 1965. He has a deep respect for its Hawaiian origins, always informing learners that they are having a session in 'Hawaiian surfboard riding'. Rusty was one of the creators of the first commercial surfboard wax and was known in the 1960s as a big wave rider. He first came to Australia on a university program and eventually immigrated here from Kauai in Hawaii.

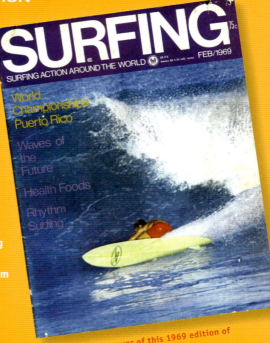

Rusty graced the cover of this 1969 edition of *Surfing* magazine.

It's not every day you have the opportunity to surf with a world champ, but to our delight, Rusty offers private lessons. But expect to learn more than just riding to shore without getting your hair wet. You'll learn about the spirit and culture of surfing and be forever captured by Rusty's thoughts on life. Find him at www.byron-bay-guide.com.au. We caught up with him at his local, the Byron Beach Café, to talk everything surf.

It all began: We lived two blocks from the main beach on the cliff overlooking the ocean in southern California and my oldest sister's job was renting surf mats. We were in the water all summer. The lifeguards took an interest in me and I borrowed their giant boards. They would take me up and down the coast to experience different waves.

Champion: I was known as a big wave rider in those days because each year I went to catch the monsters in December and January on the north shore of Oahu: Waimea, Sunset and Pipeline. After getting the most points accumulated in the 1964 season on the mainland I became the US surfing champion for 1965. That was a fun era. I had never thought of surfing as a career and went to university to become a teacher. But as I travelled and competed I realised that I had become what is now known as a 'professional surfer'.

Hawaii: I thought the Hawaiians were just magic. To me it is still the surfing capital of the world, but there are now lots of other places to enjoy and explore like Fiji, Indo, South America, the Maldives. However Hawaii to me is still the heart, in that spiritually, I believe it's still the keeper of the fire.

Rusty Miller

Surfing: Surfing is your personal interaction with the ocean. It's not just about the surfing, but about sitting on the beach afterwards talking, feeling that your body has done something. You know in surfing, you don't actually produce anything. It's just the experience and as it turns out, that is the beauty of it. It's a twist in perception about how we run our lives. I love Captain Cook's observation in the 1770s when he was walking down the beach in Hawaii and saw a man paddling to the shore on an outrigger canoe. He thought the guy had stolen something from a ship, but then he realised he was actually catching waves. He said something like, 'This guy is doing something for no reason' and to the English mind, that was baffling. Then he made this observation, 'This guy is getting great pleasure from doing nothing'.

Favourite local spot: I surf The Pass, Wategos, Lennox Head, but Lennox is my favourite. On those really big days it is my spiritual centre.

My board: I mostly ride a 10 foot Gordon and Smith SURFTECH and a 6 foot 6 inch Van Straalen fish.

Regularity: I try to go surfing each day because it is the yoga of my life that keeps me attentive to living in the present.

"Surfing is your personal interaction with the ocean. It's not just about the surfing, but about sitting on the beach afterwards talking, feeling that your body has done something."

"Rusty" Miller — Waimea Bay Hawaii — Photo by Bruce Brown Films

Bruce Brown who made Endless Summer gave me this shot from his movie Surfing Hollow Days in 1962. It was before leg ropes and the boards were without curves or a 'rocker'. The circle pattern in the wave marks that the bottom is relatively close.

Standing up

Finally! The time has arrived when learning how to surf will make you feel cool. It's time to practise on the sand. So grab your board, suck up your pride, and pay your dues – because learning how to stand up on your board is obviously a vital part of learning how to surf. Putting in practise time on the sand will really pay off when you get into the water, not to mention saving you from a few bumps and bruises. So bury those fins into the sand (to keep them from breaking), and position yourself on your board so that your feet are hanging over the edge of the tail. If you're into acting, pretend to paddle.

To stand up, place your hands on the deck just underneath your shoulders and do a quick push-up while simultaneously bringing your dominant foot under your chest and dragging your back foot over the tail. You should plant your

back foot on the stringer about a third of the way up the board and place your front foot just beyond the middle of your board.

You should make sure you are on a sand beach with small, crumbling waves. Walk until the water is about waist high. With your board pointed towards the beach, start paddling hard when a wave is 15–20 feet away from you. When you feel the wave lift you up, just repeat what you have practised on the sand. Don't think about it too much. Just do it! And don't get discouraged if it takes you a few times to stand up on your first wave – getting it the first time is about as rare as a happy Hollywood marriage. Just stick with it and savour your first surfing experience!

Board control

Having control of your board is essential. You've mastered your surfboard when you master transferring your bodyweight from foot to foot and heel to toe. Practise controlling your board on land before taking to the sea so that you become comfortable with the different manoeuvres. If you build a small mound of sand on the beach to act as the axle in a see-saw and place your board on top, you can play with shifting your body weight to your front foot.

Sure you will feel lame, but better that than flaming out right in front of, or on top of, a packed crew of hotties all jockeying madly for the best possie.

Lean your torso over your front knee to tip the nose of the board forward: this move accelerates your speed in the water. Move your upper body over your back knee to shift your weight to your back foot, lifting the nose in order to decelerate your speed on a wave.

When you get into the white water, you can practise alternating your weight from your heels to your toes to get comfortable with the body motions involved in turns. Have fun seeing how much the slightest adjustment in your weight distribution can affect your speed and position. As your surfing grows and develops, you will instinctively perfect the timing for shifting your weight on the wave.

Steering

Use your heels: used for backhand turns, turning the board away from the current direction

Use the front of your feet: used for forehand turns, turning the board in the direction you are already heading

Green = unbroken

Now that you've got control of your board, it's time to use those skills! The thrilling sense of freedom and wonder you get from steering your board across the sheer, unbroken face of a wave is what makes surfing 'green' waves so addictive. Catching unbroken waves can be a bit tricky and will take time to master, but don't get discouraged. Just remember the key to surfing green waves is coordinating the speed of your paddling and your position with the speed of the wave and the location of its breaking point. When your timing is right, you'll feel the exhilarating sensation of flying down the face of a green wave. You will feel that this brave new world is truly your own magnificent oyster ready for devouring.

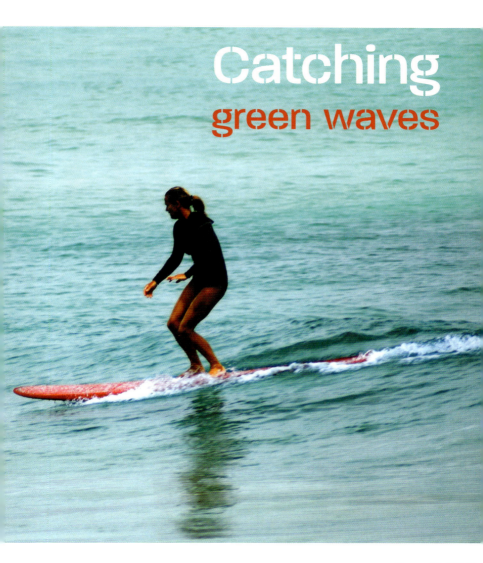

Catching
green waves

When you are sitting on your surfboard in the break zone, exhausted from paddling out and you are staring at all those wobbling bumps on the horizon, it can seem confusing to pick which wave is right for you. The best rule: keep it simple! Pick a wave you are in a position to catch and one that won't come crashing down on top of you. Translation: start small.

Here are a few more simple tips that will help you catch that perfect green wave in no time:

- When you are first learning to catch an unbroken wave, look for an uncrowded surf spot with small waves that all crumble in the same direction.

- Observe the other surfers to get a feel for how the waves are breaking. Watch which direction they go in. See what kind of rides they are catching. Learn from what they are doing.

- Paddle like a crazed lemming chasing a cliff ...

- Before you try to catch a green wave, try paddling as if you are going to catch a wave, only to pull out at the last minute. This will give you a taste for being carried on a wave and will also help you understand the speed you need to create by paddling to fully catch it.

- Now that you've mastered the timing of the swell, the only thing left to practise is the timing of the drop. A comfortable way to do this is to aim your board towards the beach for the first couple of green waves. It will feel natural to you since after the drop, the waves will break around your board and you'll end up surfing the oh-so-familiar white water. Surfing straight on a few waves will give you insight into the behaviour of the waves and get you adjusted to the feeling of the drop.

A surfer can ride a wave two different ways: forehand or backhand. Riding forehand means your body faces the wave, and it allows you to easily see how the wave is going to behave. Riding backhand is usually considered more difficult because it means your back faces the wave and you must look over your shoulder to see if the wave is going to close out on you.

Obviously, it is easier for beginners to surf on their forehand. You would have figured this out on your own, but to save you some time, here is a tip: if you are a natural footer, only ride waves that break to the right. If you are goofy footer, catch the waves that break to the left.

Eugene Tan

Surf photographer Eugene Tan estimates he has shot 115,000 images of Bondi Beach over the past nine years – that's about 35 every day. A self-confessed fanatic, he shoots everyone from groms to pros and has worked some of the most exotic, obscure and dangerous breaks the world has to offer. He also started surf website Aquabumps, a blog-style site that now has more than 30,000 daily subscribers.

On land and sea: Shooting surf from the water is really challenging for the obvious physical reasons. You not only have to know how to take the pic but you have to be physically fit as well otherwise it's quite dangerous.

Sharks: They just don't seem interested in me. I have seen them up the north coast of Australia and in Tahiti. You freak yourself out but then nothing happens. I even tried to chase them to shoot them in Tahiti and they swam underneath me but then passed by. Pics with sharks always get a lot of [web] traffic.

Near misses: I've been in the ocean a long time so you learn to judge distance well and predict a surfer's movement. I have seen a lot of them surf before so I know what they do on waves. But you can duck pretty damn quick when you need to and I've done that a lot.

Bondi: I moved here about 12 years ago and I love it. It's such an interesting place with a lot going on. It's amazing that such a busy suburb is so close to surfable waves. Bondi waves are not world class, but they are good enough to enjoy – and to have the urban landscape right there by the break is quite unique. Travelling a bit now, I've started to realise how uncommon that is.

As a surfer: I'm one of three boys and we all started body surfing when we were about three and as soon as we could stand on a board, we were on our way.

Surfing is so peaceful: It's pretty hard to be stressed out there. All of my friends are hot surfers who are a lot better than me so I never once considered competition.

Favourite surf spot: Would have to be Hollow Trees in Indonesia. It has it all, a perfect break, perfect sun, perfect clear water, perfect barrels, an idyllic beach ... it's all there. But it's so damn hard to get to. It would take two days to get there if we left from Sydney now.

Favourite personal shot: They change all the time. At the moment it's a black and white shot of an angry shore break against a cliff. The background is black and the waves are frothing up, but there's no surfer in it. It was on a beach that was normally flat so it was a surprise shot.

The craft: There is so much to photography; it's challenging. Every day is different down at the beach. This morning there was a huge pink strip of clouds going vertical and that was a surprise so it makes things interesting. Different light, wave heights, winds, people, conditions ... there's always something interesting and new to shoot.

Escapism: I started Aquabumps about nine years ago before anyone really knew what blogging was. There are a lot of people that spend their whole day behind a desk. That little [daily] update from Aquabumps with pics and info provides a little window to the outside world. It's a two-minute slice of the beach each day, a nice escape. People kind of daydream a bit when it arrives before they get back to work.

"There is so much to photography; it's challenging. Every day is different down at the beach."

The best? I'm not sure I'm the best surf photographer, but I'm perhaps one of the most fanatical. Some days I'm sitting on a beach in the morning and it's 5 degrees and I am wondering what the hell I'm doing there, but you just never know what might happen. You always get good shots when you think nothing will happen.

Favourite to shoot: I've shot most of the top 44 surfers in the world, but Taj Burrows would have to be my pick. He is electric. He is fast and I struggle to keep up with him sometimes.

Check him out: www.aquabumps.com

This pic is called 'Mirror Wave' and was shot in Fiji. The water is just incredible there — so clear and blue.

One of my fave shots ever (that took me seven years to capture!)
of Bondi Beach, Sydney – Eugene

The term 'lineup' refers to the calm area in the water just beyond the breaking point where surfers sit and wait to catch their waves. It can be an intimidating place for a beginner surfer. However, a simple understanding of the anatomy of the beach coupled with basic surf etiquette can help ease those nerves and will allow you to concentrate on surfing and not just your vulnerable surfer ego!

Experienced surfers use the rip (an area of water where the waves aren't breaking) to paddle out to the lineup for two logical reasons: it saves you wasting valuable energy battling with the white water and it also means you'll stay out of the path of other surfers riding waves.

Observe the pathways of other surfers in the water, and you'll more than likely find the easiest path out to the lineup. And once you get there, remember to follow the ancient rules of surfing that the Hawaiians have passed down for generations: if you share a wave with someone of the opposite sex, you can get down and dirty in the sand afterwards. Well, try it on for size and see how you go anyway. Oh, and the unwritten rule that says beginner surfers must wait their turn!

Am I ready for the lineup?

You're ready to face the lineup when you can stand relatively well in the white water and feel confident that you can paddle well enough to get out of someone's way.

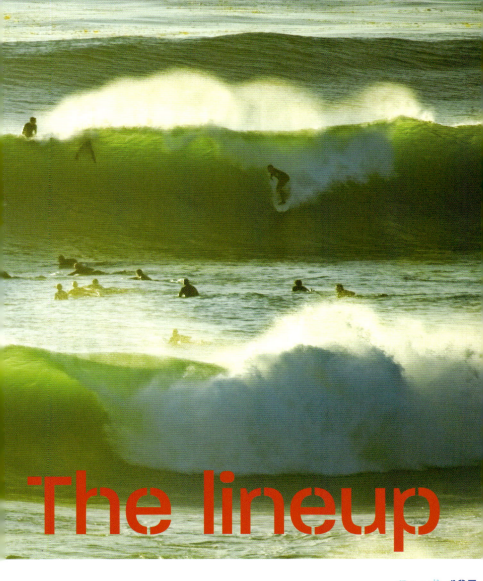

The lineup

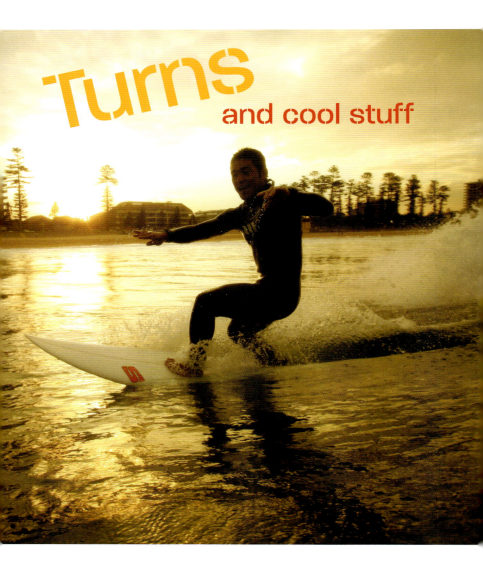

Turns
and cool stuff

Ready for a turn? Making actual turns on your surfboard is a great achievement in your surfing. The exhilaration you will feel from manipulating movements from a wave that you're flying across on your board comes from your newfound sense of control. Learning to turn means you now have the ability to express your own personal style of surfing, and you also have the ability to avoid a surfer-on-surfer collision in the water.

You can practise moving up and down the face of an unbroken wave by transferring your body weight between your front and back foot.

By now you will hopefully have noticed that with greater speed comes greater stability. It is your ability to control speed that will allow you to make beautiful, outrageously exhilarating turns. Not to mention that it will officially erase the word 'liability' all beginners have stamped across their foreheads as they go speeding uncontrollably down the face of a wave. So practise and have fun with it!

And when it comes to turning, every surfer has an important decision to make while paddling for a wave: either aim your board towards the beach, take the drop straight down the face of the wave and make a bottom turn to begin your ride on the wave, or paddle at an angle so that when you pop up your ride has already begun across the face of the wave. As you will soon discover, both have their advantages and both contribute to getting a good ride full of bottom turns, cutbacks, re-entries and maybe even a floater. So what are those, you ask?

The bottom turn, a U-shaped turn you make at the bottom of the wave on your inside rail, can make or break your ride. As 2000 world champion Sunny Garcia said, 'Without a good bottom turn you have nothing'. Many great surfers perfected this essential move and carved their place in the pantheon of all-time heroes — names such as Phil Edwards, Nat Young, Jeff Hakman, not to mention the man regarded as the greatest executor of all, Hawaiian Barry Kanaiaupuni.

All beginners should tackle the forehand bottom turn before the backhand, unless you consider yourself some sort of kamikaze. And if you are that type of person, that is okay too, because the idea of both the forehand and backhand bottom turn is to become a speed freak. You're aiming to utilise the speed gained from your drop and the momentum of the water speeding up the face of the wave. Here's a quick step by step:

1. Drop in with your board aimed towards the beach, leaning back slightly to keep your weight over your back foot.

2. At the bottom of the wave, lean in towards the face of the wave, using your front arm to point in the direction you want to go: up the face of the wave.

3. As your body begins to untwist and your board begins to turn, gently lean your weight forward to help steer your board up the wave and complete the end of your 'U'.

4. Redistribute your weight evenly, and decide whether to ride the face of the wave or go into a top turn.

For a backhand bottom turn, follow the same steps, except you must lean on your heels, look over your shoulder, and drop your front arm to the water to act as a pivot point. In a backhand bottom turn, your lower body performs most of the work.

Bottom turns

The forehand cutback is a horseshoe-shaped turn that begins on the shoulder of the wave and arcs back down to the base of the wave, allowing the surfer to remain close to the wave's source of power. It's a tricky move that takes a lot of practise to perfect and it's best to watch it in a live sequence to really understand what to do. Many of the great surfers throughout history were particularly renowned for their cutback. Nat Young's 1966 World Contest win was largely confirmed on the back of his aggressive cutback, which completely outclassed the noseriding and subtle trimming of the other contestants.

Cutbacks are handy to keep you from flying over the back of the wave and to drop off extra speed you have built up with the manoeuvre. Use these guidelines to help complete the turn:

1. Bend your knees to keep your centre of gravity low, applying weight to your heels and leaning on your outside rail.

2. Look to where you want to go, shift most of your weight to your back heel, and swing your front arm around the back of your body. Remember to keep your eyes on the curl of the wave and envision a smooth horseshoe-shaped turn.

3. When you reach the base of the wave, readjust your body weight to centre yourself, and pull out of the turn by leaning on your inside rail.

You may notice that the backhand cutback is easier to complete because you are already facing the direction of the turn. Just transfer your weight to your toes when you are on the shoulder of the wave, bend your knees, turn your upper body towards the direction you want to go, and lean over your inside rail – hard. The speed and sharpness of your turn depends on how hard you lean over your board. You can drop your back arm to the water to act as a pivot point and provide you with some extra stability if you need to.

After some time in the water, you will begin to notice similarities between the motions of a bottom turn and a cutback.

Cutbacks

To generate maximum power when surfing and to utilise the entire face of the wave, a surfer needs to surf a wave from top to bottom. A critical manoeuvre is the re-entry turn: a high speed vertical climb up the face of the wave coupled with a sharp turn to re-enter or drop down the face of the wave. This tricky move takes some serious confidence but will elevate your surfer status immediately!

Twisting your body is key to this move, so channel the power of the Beatles, twist your little heart out, and follow these tips.

1. Crouch low and twist your torso to aim high on the wave face, allowing your lower body to complete your bottom turn while your upper body prepares for your re-entry.

2. Transfer your body weight to your heels, apply pressure to your back foot, and point with your front hand to the base of the wave. Keep your eyes focused on the point of the wave where you want your board to end up.

3. As you come back down the face of the wave, make sure to keep pressure on your back foot to avoid nose diving. You can either pull out of the descent down the wave face and ride on the middle of the wave, or descend to the wave base and go into another bottom turn.

In a backhand re-entry, you will already be facing the direction of the turn. As you come out of your backhand bottom turn and travel up the face of the wave, remember to keep your lower body and your upper body independent of each other so the lower body can complete the turn while the upper body twists to prepare for the next step. When you reach the top of the wave, twist your torso to look back towards the bottom of the wave and point with your front arm in the direction you want to go. Transfer your weight to the outside rail, and the force of the breaking lip along with gravity will swing your board around under you. When you reach the base of the wave, re-centre your weight and bend your knees to absorb the impact.

Re-entry

A floater is an angled climb from the bottom of a wave to the top, where you glide along the top for a bit before coming down the face again. You see this when waves are closing out and a surfer wants to bypass this and keep going as the wave reforms, or wants to bypass a specific section of a wave. You usually head up the wave at a 45-degree angle. It's a pretty flashy move so if you manage it, you should be damn proud of yourself.

The aim is to glide laterally across the white water of the lip before dropping back down again. Stick to the small crumbling waves when perfecting this manoeuvre to avoid broken ankles, a broken board or a broken spirit.

Here's how to do it: When you are coming out of a bottom turn and riding up the face of a wave, instead of going into a top turn, go up and onto the oncoming white water section. Bend your knees, widen your stance, and keep low and centred over your board. As in the re-entry, gravity and the force of the wave will do most of the work for you in your descent. If you can time your floater right, the lip will land right before you, providing a nice cushion of white water for your landing.

The move is often credited to the late Aussie surfer Mark Sainsbury, the 1986 world amateur champion, but he merely perfected what a lot of others had been trying and occasionally pulling off since the late 1970s. It is a rarity in waves over 10 feet but the manoeuvre led the way to other radical moves championed by Kelly Slater and other 'new school' surfers who came onto the scene in the early 1990s.

The floater is a bit like surfing's version of Whacko Jacko's moonwalk, except way cooler, more rewarding, and unlikely to be butchered at suburban discos. Just don't try it in front of a packed house until you've mastered your act off the main stage.

Floaters

Wipe

A wipeout is usually a pretty spectacular fall that causes you and your board to plunge into the wave like you've just been thrown into a tumble dryer. Unfortunately, it will happen often ... but as they say, 'if you wipe out, at least you know you've gone for it'.

outs

You will also know you are alive after surviving three sets of waves on the head with a belly full of water and other surfers nearly decapitating you with their fins. But accentuate the positive: the cardio workout is fantastic! Accept that even great surfers wipe out and give in to the fact that an aquatic hammering can sometimes be a liberating experience and you can now claim membership of 'the brethren'.

Tips for
wipeouts

- First relax and breathe, counting to three before you do anything.

- Read the tension on your leg rope. If there is no pressure, your board is most likely above you. If there's a huge amount of tension, be aware that your board might be getting ready to smack you in the head. In either case, use your hands to protect your head from the board swinging back or to stop you from surfacing underneath the board and its fins.

- Try to fall to the back of the board into the face or the back of a wave, instead of forward into the wave's impact and the direction of the board.

- Don't drop your hands from your head until you have surfaced and can clearly see where you are and where the board is.

- Never dive down headfirst as the water could be shallow.

- Try to be calm as the resurface can take a while and you don't want to use oxygen unnecessarily.

- Go with the water flow, gently resurfacing, laughing, and going again.

Midget Farrelly

Bernard 'Midget' Farrelly is a legend of the sport, renowned for his 1964 world championship win in front of a home crowd at Manly Beach. He is also considered one of the world's finest board shapers and manufacturers. He started surfing in the 1950s and has watched the sport come and go.

It all began: After visiting Wales, Canada and New Zealand in 1955 where we tried to surf an ironing board, I found an old board washed up after a storm on Manly Beach and so I jumped it. I was 11 at the time.

"The perfect surf is every time. You can go in feeling crappy and you come out feeling sensational ..."

Surfing evolution: Surfing has had a lot of stops and starts. The biggest start was in '64 when fathers started buying their daughters boards so they could go to the beach after school but the sport crashed in the late 60s and 70s before reviving again in the 70s. There were new people, new styles of surfing and a new format for competition. Unfortunately it flatlined again in the 80s in the earring, tattoos and designer boards period, only to resurface in the 90s with longboards, bodyboards, surf schools and board hire. And now it's on one of the highest highs we have seen. There are squillions of people learning to surf and our guys and girls are doing so well on the circuit. It's a whole new thing.

Best competition moment: I wasn't really ever conscious of it and I had been told by my enemies for so long that I was no good but when I look back at the events of '64 I think, 'Oh actually, that wasn't too bad'. Twenty years on, I now appreciate it.

Perfect surf: The perfect surf is every time. You can go in feeling crappy and you come out feeling sensational because you get some oxygen into your blood, you stretch your muscles, you've meditated and it doesn't matter if it's one foot, triple overhead or 15 feet, you come out a different person.

Surf heroes: Everyone who did something that I couldn't. You learn from everyone else because there is always someone out there who can do something that you can't. Everyone gives you something.

Favourite spot: Any old crappy beach really. As long as you're out there.

Shark encounter: There was one close call but he was at least three waves away.

Injuries: The worst was four stitches behind my ear.

No-no: There are many things you shouldn't do, an obvious one is not going too far out of your zone.

4.

Surf rules and safe

FIRST AID KIT

ety

There are a few surfing safety tips, rules and unwritten laws that you must abide by. Read any surfing magazine or spend time with a few surfers and you'll realise that respect in the water is a big thing and nothing gets a surfer more annoyed than someone misbehaving. Here are a few tips which will help you — but overall, use commonsense and courtesy as you would on land.

Surf etiquette

There are some simple rules that it's best to stick to when surfing – not only for manners' sake, but also simply to be safe:

- **Be aware of other people in the water.** It's best to avoid clusters of people or other surfers initially, until you learn to control yourself better and also get acquainted with the dos and don'ts of surfing. The key is to be aware of who is around you at all times to avoid any collisions or mishaps.

- **Don't catch a wave and then turn straight back around.** Instead, paddle out wide of where the waves are breaking so you avoid incoming surfers.

- **Never drop in.** I might say that again. Never drop in on someone. It's easier said than done, but essentially it means this: the person closest to the breaking wave has priority to ride it. Stick to this rule if you want friends out there. The few kind-hearted surfers left after seeing you drop in may put it down to beginner's nerves and offer you a gentle word of instruction. But the nastier repercussions of this transgression could follow you up the sand, out of the car park and even mark you as a dreaded drop-in forever. So kiddies, it's simple: DON'T!

- **Wait your turn in the lineup.** Snaking (paddling around surfers in the lineup who have been waiting their turn) so that you can catch the next wave is just as bad as dropping in. Or maybe it's worse, because it's premeditated. Don't do it.

- **As a beginner, avoid the lineup** until you are confident you can do controlled takeoffs.

- **Never paddle out to the lineup through the impact zone** (where the waves are breaking and people are surfing), or where people are in the middle of catching waves. You'd never walk into traffic, would you?

- **When paddling out, a surfer riding the wave always has right of way.** And don't paddle too close to another surfer – those fins will cut you like meat cleavers if a wave suddenly throws them in your face.

- **Respect the beach's local**s if you are a visitor or newcomer. Behave like a guest in someone's home.

- **Don't be a wave hog.** Make sure you share! This seems funny but it can cause real problems, especially if you are new to the area. You may be 'influenced' to surf fresh real estate if you don't.

- **Respect more seasoned surfers than yourself.** Have you heard of the old saying 'respect your elders'?

- **Try and control your board.** This is where a leg rope comes in handy, especially if you are struggling to keep a rein on it. Never, never, ever throw your board away before looking behind and around you to ensure no one is near you. Someone could get killed.

Martin Grose

Martin Grose is the National Development Manager of Surfing Australia. He's also a mad keen surfer, father of two and an all-round nice guy.

Times have changed: Surfing in Australia has become an iconic

sport – everyone wants to try it and so they should. Everyone wants to share in the feeling. Not so many years back it was just a few individuals out there surfing the waves and they were looked upon as perhaps not the most respected people in the community at the time, but it's funny how things turn out. It was those guys who were behind one of the biggest moves in sport we have seen.

Surfing in Australia: We have embraced surfing because of our

coastal lifestyle and while we have hero world champions, we also have hero board builders, shapers and manufacturers. Surfing is now interwoven into the fabric of Australian life. For some it's a competitive world while for others it's getting together with your mates and having a good time. When I'm in the water I don't think about anything but getting another wave. It's selfish, but it's fun.

Respect nature: When we surf, we appreciate the jewels and gems

that the ocean offers. You love it and challenge it but you must also respect it on the days that it rears its ugly head. When we work with nature, we can dance with it, but don't try to lead it too much because someone might tread on your toes.

"When I'm in the water I don't think about anything but getting another wave. It's fun."

Listen up:
don't drop in!

Dropping in on someone is the worst thing you can do as a new surfer. Lots of people get confused about it, but really it's just like jumping a queue, you move in to steal the wave when the person right beside you was next in line. How do you tell? The surfer closest to the break of the wave has right of way.

Surf safe tips

These seem pretty obvious I must admit, but seeing you're not on land, take note. These are tips for us all, beginners to the most experienced surfers.

- Don't mix surfing and alcohol. Save the drinking for the after-surf brag session. You may feel groovy, man, letting loose on the juice, but your vision, balance and timing will be out, which is not only dangerous but will stymie whatever style you have acquired in your short time surfing.

- Avoid surfing until at least 30 minutes after a meal.

- Don't surf alone – even when you are good!

- Keep our beaches clean. Remember, you're sharing the beach with marine and plant life, not just other surfers and swimmers.

- Don't surf (or swim) at night.

- Consider a helmet if surfing near rocks.

- If you get into difficulty, keep your board close as it's your rescue flotation device.

- Have fun but never at the expense of others in the water.

- Always stretch.

- Be mindful of suffering from the extremes of dehydration and hypothermia. Always carry water with you for the former and for the latter, if you start to experience intense shivering, get out and get help.

Where's my stuff?

Unfortunately stuff gets stolen from beaches all the time. When surfing you have a few options:

1. Lock it in your car and either hide the key or use the key compartment of your wetsuit (if you're wearing one). If you hide the key under the car, make sure no one is watching.

2. Leave it on the beach. Stuff your key and valuables in the bottom of your bag and monitor it from the surf. Get a bright bag or towel so it's easy to spot and if you do this, take as few valuables as possible to the beach to minimise the risk.

3. Get someone else on the beach (or a friend) to watch it. This works fine, unless you tend to associate with kleptomaniacs.

4. Take the butler on a day trip and promise him a special treat for his ad hoc security work.

Looking after yourself

As well as looking after your stuff, it's also wise to look after yourself. Some of these things are obvious, but there are quite a few nasties out there so it's best to be prepared.

Be sunsmart

We all love the sun, duh, but don't let it kill you. Aussies have the highest rate of skin cancer in the world with one in two people who grow up on our luscious shores developing some form of skin cancer, according to the NSW Cancer Council. The most important way to reduce your risk of skin cancer is to avoid getting sunburnt. Pink skin, and even a tan, is a sign of skin cell damage which can lead to skin cancer. Remember – there is no such thing as a healthy tan.

You can minimise your exposure by avoiding surfing or being out in the sun during peak UV times between 10 am and 2 pm (11 am–3 pm during daylight savings time), however, the best waves won't always fit in with this.

Follow the NSW Cancer Council's five easy ways to be SunSmart:

1. **Cover up (slip):** When you're in the water, wear a rash vest to cover the exposed upper body (the longer the sleeves the better), but when out of the water, chuck on some clothes, a shirt, sarong or towel.

2. **Smother yourself (slop):** Always use SPF30+ broad spectrum, water resistant sunscreen before you go for a surf, and make sure you reapply it every two hours. Sunscreen does not provide 100 per cent protection from the sun, but slopping it on is one of the best ways you can protect yourself from harmful rays.

3. **Shade up (slap):** Wear a hat between surfs. It's a bit hard in the water, but when you're out of the waves, relaxing on the beach or having breakfast or lunch after a session, wear a wide-brimmed hat that shades your neck and face. There are plenty on offer for girls and some hip straw options now available for guys.

4. **Protect your eyes:** Wear sunnies when you're out of the water.

5. **Stick under the trees and umbrellas:** When hanging on the beach between surfs, stay in the shade as much as possible.

Don't miss these vital places when smothering up with sunscreen: the tops of your hands and feet, under your chin, the back of your neck, the parting in your hair.

Other nasties to look out for

Surfing comes with a few nasties that can cause you trouble, whether in the water or on land, either here or as you venture out to more remote surfing locations.

Here's a summary of the most common, and what to do about them.

Angry locals

Not always easy to spot straight off, the POOL (Pissed Off Older Local) nevertheless has certain universal traits distinguishable at any surf spot: the stink-eye greeting to anyone not in his immediate circle in the lineup, which declares his or her love of all humanity, newcomers and indeed surfing in general. The mumbled obscenities that gradually mount to an audible roar at perceived interlopers and 'kooks'. Take note here students, as interlopers or kooks simply mean anyone that moved here after him ... so don't fret, just keep out of his way. Observe his mounting frustration at having to actually paddle and fight for waves he deems his by right of surf time logged or his parents' address. Finally, the ugly realisation etched on his face that his best days are passed, a new generation of hotties has claimed the throne and he simply isn't having fun anymore.

Bluebottles

These guys are common on Australian beaches, especially around Bondi. They are a blue jellyfish with a long tail that has a way of getting tangled around your limbs. They drift on the surface and sometimes are washed ashore. Most lifeguards will warn you if they are around. They can give you a nasty sting, which, if you're asthmatic or allergic, can be serious, causing respiratory distress.

Action: Wash off any tentacles with sea water, immerse in warm or hot water, then apply ice. If you have a reaction, specifically respiratory trouble, see a doctor, lifesaver or lifeguard. Note: some people say peeing on it works. Can't say I've tried it.

Blue-ringed octopus

A tentacle-clad creature that grows to around 12 cm long, the blue-ringed octopus lives in shallow waters and rock pools around the Australian coast. This little devil is named for the small blue spots that appear on its body when threatened. While the bite is relatively painless, the impact is deadly and you must seek immediate medical assistance. Symptoms include difficulty breathing and swallowing, blurred vision, a numb tongue and lips.

Action: Immobilise the wound with a bandage if you have one and get medical help, fast. Be aware that you may have to perform CPR.

Seasnakes

As differentiated from the previously mentioned, and deadly if not castigated, seasnakes are actually quite harmless to surfers despite being fatal if a bite occurs, and few will ever see them. More than anything, these guys are curious – so if you do see one, he'll probably have a good look around before he takes off.

Action: If bitten, immobilise the wound and seek medical assistance immediately.

Sea urchins

These guys are the black, spiky, needle-like buggers that infest nooks and crannies of rocky outcrops at point and reef breaks. Not only do they hurt when stepped on, they break off in your flesh, are difficult to get out (think scalpel and tweezers ... ouch!) and if left to fester can poison your bloodstream and prove even more painful. But think positively: if you do butcher an urchin via your blind little tap dance, there is a way to get revenge on the sucker. Salvage its inner flesh and turn a profit by selling it to a Japanese connoisseur for big bucks.

Action: Immerse the limb in warm or hot water and it's best to see a doctor to remove any parts of the spine. Don't try and do it yourself.

Stingrays

Stingrays are a kind of fish covered in cartilage, and they're common in coastal waters. Although they've got a pretty mean sting on them, they aren't particularly aggressive, and are more likely to swim away than sting you. But as some of these critters can grow up to 14 feet long, they can certainly scare you! If you are stung, it's painful and there is, of course, a chance it can kill you if you're stung in a vital organ. You'll feel intense burning, struggle with your breathing, and suffer numbness around the wound.

Action: Immerse the wound with warm or hot water, and get medical help immediately. Don't try and remove the barb yourself.

Bullrout and stonefish

These fish are more common in tropical waters but can be found in rocky beaches. They are camouflaged and have super-sharp and poisonous spines on their back. If stung, you'll have immediate and acute pain. Sometimes the actual spine will remain in the wound.

Action: Pour warm liquid over the wound repeatedly, removing any part of the fish, and get medical help, fast.

Snakes

You'll rarely find any here, but as you begin to surf further afield, you may encounter a snake on a grassy track. If you come across a snake, simply give it some space or go around it. Mostly, it will be just as surprised to see you as you are to see it. However, if you are bitten ...

Action: Keep as still as possible. Don't wash or play with the wound in any way. Instead, bandage the wound firmly, covering it well (the bandage should spread 15 cm across the bite). If possible, use wood or a stick to splint the limb to immobilise it (which slows down the blood flow) and get to hospital immediately. If possible, identify the snake in case an antivenin is needed, or if it's deceased, bring it along.

Unsure of a bite? If you or a friend starts to vomit or feel nauseous, have abdominal pain, b_urred vision or severe headaches, you may have been bitten. Look around for the snake or the bite.

Spiders

As with snakes, spiders are common problems for surfers who go further afield in bush tracks mainly. The funnel-web and the redback cause most problems, and both are found here! The funnel-web is a large, black, reddish-brown spider, while the redback has a red strip on its back. Symptoms are similar for both. You'll feel intense pain at the bite, abdominal pain, nausea, and difficulty breathing. You'll sweat, your muscles will feel weak and you may experience cold shivers or spasms.

Action (funnel web): Immobilise and splint the wound and get medical help, fast.

Action (red back): Apply ice or a cold pack and get medical help.

The big ones – sharks

While just over one person dies from shark attacks in Australian waters each year, surfers must acknowledge that by being in the water, they are at risk. Most seasoned surfers don't fear sharks, but they do respect them. Many say that sharks will only attack when they are old and mistake you for their usual prey. However, there are three types of sharks which are known to attack: the bull shark, the great white and the tiger shark.

If you are surfing and you see a shark, you must:

- try to remain calm, and
- attempt to leave the area as quickly and quietly as possible.

If an attack is imminent:

- try to keep your eye on the shark at all times
- attempt to hit the shark's nose or gouge its eyes, and
- put your board between you and it.

How to avoid shark attacks:

- Don't surf with open wounds of any sort. If you cut yourself, paddle in. Did you know that some sharks can detect a drop of blood as little as one part per million from up to a kilometre away? Reassuring, isn't it?
- Never surf in the dark or at dusk as this is their main feeding time.
- Avoid surfing near river mouths where sharks lurk looking for debris and creatures from the river.

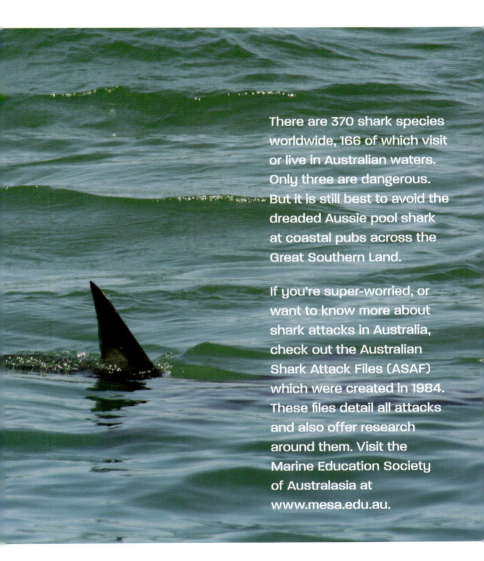

There are 370 shark species worldwide, 166 of which visit or live in Australian waters. Only three are dangerous. But it is still best to avoid the dreaded Aussie pool shark at coastal pubs across the Great Southern Land.

If you're super-worried, or want to know more about shark attacks in Australia, check out the Australian Shark Attack Files (ASAF) which were created in 1984. These files detail all attacks and also offer research around them. Visit the Marine Education Society of Australasia at www.mesa.edu.au.

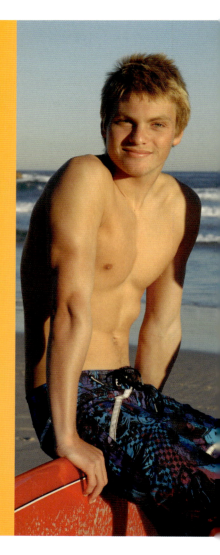

Perth Standlick

Bondi lad Perth Standlick rode his first wave at the age of seven. Thanks to his aggressive style, he has been on the radar as one of Australia's potential next great surfers since his debut on the competitive circuit. Perth is currently on the junior pro tour and hopes to move up the chain in the future. We took a surf with Perth (okay, we watched) in Bondi to talk about his future and living in Bondi.

Local: I grew up in Bondi and I've surfed here all my life. I love to travel, but this will always be home.

Start: I caught my first wave when I was seven in Byron Bay actually, but really got into surfing at the age of 10. I was watching the surf and I thought 'I'd like to try that' and the next minute, I was in the water.

Right now: I'm travelling around doing the pro juniors in Australia, just trying to do as well as I can and make a name for myself and hopefully earn as much money as I can so I don't have to do too much work! I can't wait to start travelling the world and surfing better waves.

Training: I do a fair bit of fitness training outside of the water, working on my core strength, doing lots of soft sand runs.

Surf favourites: I love to watch Joel Parkinson, he's the smoothest surfer, and Bobby Martinez is pretty good. I have plenty of favourites but they are the two main ones at the moment.

Injuries: I've had a couple, torn muscles mainly. I hurt my knee quite badly a couple of years ago and have broken my collar bone.

Not a surfer: If I wasn't a surfer, I'd probably be a nerd. I'm not really good at anything else and apart from surfing, I am quite uncoordinated.

Bondi: The surf's pretty bad here, the waves can be quite terrible, but it's great for learning because it's a mellow easy wave and it's usually quite crowded so you are never on your own. There's always someone to talk to and ask for instructions out in the water. As for Bondi generally, I love living here. There are so many different people from all around the world and it's so good to meet new people, all the travellers.

Your medical kit

If you are going to take surf a little more seriously than surfing a softie at populated beach breaks, you should create a medical kit to take with you, just in case. You can grab them from chemists or a range of surfing organisations like Surfing Australia.

Your kit should include:

- bandages, cotton balls, gauze and sterile dressings
- painkillers
- gloves and disinfectant
- Scissors and tweezers
- a knife and some safety pins
- saline water and antiseptic cream, and
- a massage therapist to soothe your bruised ego during your interminable learning curve.

KIT

Basic
first aid
for surfers

Unfortunately you will get hurt at some time in your surfing life, sometimes badly, but mostly if you're smart and careful it'll just be cuts and bruising. For those times when you're not so smart ... or perhaps the surf seems to be working against you, here's some advice from Surf Life Saving Australia on what to do when you're injured.

- **Bleeding (we have a bleeder, people):** Most bleeding is superficial, easily recognised, relatively minor in quantity and easily stopped (phew). However, bleeding from an artery looks different: the flow is brisk and spurting. If you have an arterial bleed, you need to get help. While you're waiting for help to arrive, give the wound immediate attention by applying pressure. If the bleed is on a limb that does not seem to be broken, elevate it.

- **Cuts and abrasions:** You'll get plenty of these but they're easily fixed. Clean any dirt with soap and water, and if you have it, sterile saline (fresh water that has salt in it). Apply pressure to stop bleeding, then cover it with a sterile non-stick dressing. If the cut is deep or you're worried about it in any way, seek medical attention.

- **Fin Chop:** If you receive a serious fin chop and are wearing a wetsuit, leave it on because it will apply compression. If not, squeeze the wound together and get help.

- **Bleeding from the nose:** Yes it does happen. Place your hand over the soft part of your nostrils and apply pressure for up to 10 minutes or until bleeding stops. Breathe through your mouth and don't blow or sniff through the nose until bleeding stops. If bleeding doesn't stop after 10 minutes, seek medical help.

- **Surfer's cramp:** Surfers can get a painful muscle spasm (often in their calves) as a result of dehydration. Float for a bit on your board or beside your board and move your legs around for relief, stretching your leg and foot out as far as possible. You should head for the shore for a drink of water. If you want to keep surfing but the pain persists, you'll need to go in, sit on your bottom and stretch the leg – even if the set was too good to abandon! Drink warm drinks if the cramp was caused by cold water or a cold drink if it was caused by warm water.

- **Sunburn:** Get yourself to a cool, shady place and if it's really bad, cool the sunburn for at least 20 minutes with cold water. Drink plenty of fluid and do not prick any blisters. If you feel nauseous, start vomiting or have severe headaches you should seek medical help.

- **Bone or ligament injuries, sprains and strains:** Rest, Ice, Compress and Elevate (RICE) are the tricks of the trade for these surfers' woes. Lie down and take a break, put ice or cold packs on the affected area, wrap a compression bandage (or something similar if that's all you have) around the injured limb to support and restrict movement, and support the limb so it's above the level of your heart.

If the injuries are of a more serious nature, especially spinal injuries, grab a lifeguard or seek medical assistance if the beach is not patrolled.

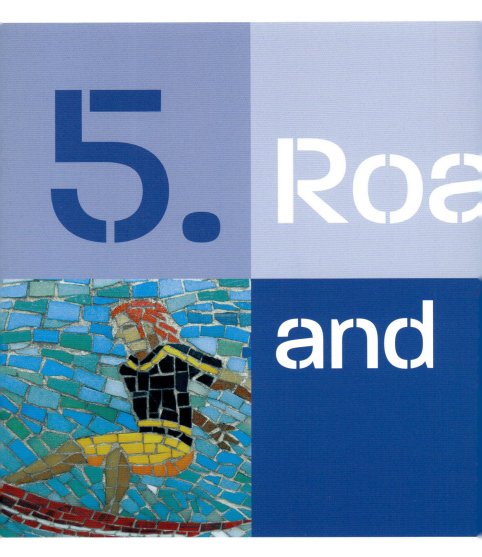

5. Roa and

d trips

hot spots

So now you know the basics, it's time to get on the road ...

Ah, the smells of the road trip – salty air, burning rubber, petrol, other gaseous odours – just thinking about it is enough to make you grab your board and hit the blacktop. As Barton Lynch says, 'Getting in the car with your mates, hitting the road, searching for waves, and hoping you are going to score is one of the best things about the surf culture'. And although spontaneity adds to the excitement of a surf safari, an unplanned road trip can be about as fun as an unplanned pregnancy. So here are a few tips:

Bank your days – Your mates will never let you live down the day you said no to a surf trip just because you couldn't take time off work. Use the flat days when the waves aren't good to work and get your commitments out of the way, so when it's going off, you can blow off work and go surf. And for that matter, use your time at work to do research on your destination. For better or for worse, the internet has revolutionised the surf safari, so use it. You don't want to surf somewhere that's a bit dodgy to find out the next beach is brilliant.

Use protection – Clearly, your board is the most important part of your equipment, so don't end the adventure before it evens starts by letting it get dinged up (it could even break!). The fins are the most vulnerable part of your board when you're travelling, so take care to pack them properly. If they are removable, wrap them in a towel – just don't forget to pack your fin key! The easiest way to protect non-removable fins is to buy a fin protector or fin box, although you can make your own from polystyrene blocks (electrical warehouses hand these out for free). Next, use a little extra padding for the fins and rails because they are more likely to get damaged than the deck and bottom of the board. If your car is jammed or you're travelling a long way, the risk of your board getting damaged is much higher. Get hold of some foam pipe insulation, slice the tube on one side, pop it on your rails, and secure with shrinkwrap. Lastly, invest in a good board bag at least 10 mm thick – although a hard travel case would be ideal. Shove some towels or clothing into the bag for some extra padding, double check to make sure nothing hard (like a leg rope) is inside the board bag, and you are good to go.

Double down – Take two boards in case one snaps. Pack a spare leg rope, a first aid kit, a board repair kit (it's amazing what can happen to them in transit), wax, a wax comb, and your sunscreen. Don't risk wasting the trip by not packing spares – two is always better than one.

Check the wheels man – Never trust any of your prospective surf travellers when they tell you, 'Yeah maaate, the '71 Holden is goin' great guns. Don't worry, the beast is sweet mate!' All surfers can tell of precious surf safari time wasted stuck at a hick-town mechanic's for the old wagon to get rebooted. Not securing the best possible wheels to travel in will not only be uncomfortable and limit your wave potential, it could prove fatal on Australia's less than autobahn-like highways. A word of warning though: if you're gonna nick the keys to Dad's hot rod you had better plan on surfing a very secret spot, eh?

Maverick and Goose – If you want to still be on speaking terms with your mates at the end of the trip, take a few pointers from Top Gun. The wingman is a crucial role – you have the iPod to manage, maps to read, and the all-important job of keeping the driver awake and entertained with your dirtiest jokes. Leave the sleeping for the backseat.

Respect – It's the most important thing in the water (and in life really). So don't let travelling be your excuse to start dropping in or snaking waves. Respect the customs and rights of the local surfers. You don't have to forfeit your own right to a wave, just maintain a basic level of etiquette. If you act like an ass, not only will one or more locals probably force you into a bad session, but you'll also be responsible for giving fellow travellers a rank reputation. And you may just be run out of town, so tread lightly.

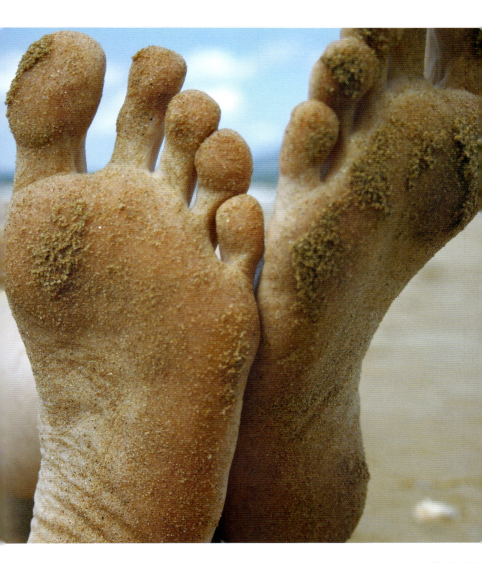

A quick chat ...

with DEREK RECIO of Tracks Magazine

Memories of my first wave: Being pushed onto what I thought was a biggie wave by my old man.

Why I love it: The lifestyle, fitness, and it's so much fun.

Surfing in Australia: The change in the last 50 or so years had been massive. There are so many people in the water these days, especially at the city beaches. It's great to see so many people out there having fun but it can get pretty hectic! The pros are ripping and the Aussies are a force to be reckoned with. Got to love that.

Surfing tips: Respect the locals of the beach. Start somewhere that's not crowded or where other beginners are. Learn the rules and be aware of what is going on around you. Don't get too big for your boots and don't get in other people's way, especially locals. Learn to duck dive 'cause bailing your board can really piss off people around you!

Best thing you can do as a surfer: Get barrelled.

Worst thing you can do as a surfer: Litter. It ends up in the ocean, people!

Favourite surf spot: Treasure Island, Banyaks. Three barrels a wave if you're lucky.

Should you be afraid of sharks? Yes, it's too crowded out there these days. Only joking.

Best piece of surfing advice you were ever given:
Why don't you duck dive? I learned that day thanks to a huge set.

Surfing heroes: Joel Parkinson, Bruce Irons, Kelly Slater.

Love surfing: Ripping on a good wave is the best feeling.

First wipeout, how did you feel? Rattled.

Message to any new surfer: Take it easy, please!

Hot surf spots in
Australia

Australia has literally thousands of surfing spots from the scary to the gentle, from the family-friendly to the territorial and freaky. Here we list some good spots for beginners. For more comprehensive guides and for spots for intermediate to experienced surfers, visit sites like www.thesurferstravelguide.com.au.

Lakes Entrance

New South Wales

Bondi Beach, Sydney: There are lots of people (40,000 on a summer's day) but the northern end almost always offers up good surf for beginners.

Manly Beach: A long sandy-bottomed beach with multiple breaks.

Clarkes Beach, Byron Bay: Perfect conditions 90 per cent of the time. Gentle waves which offer a surprisingly long ride. Plenty of other beaches nearby if you are feeling confident.

Seven Mile Beach, Lennox Head: Just south of Byron Bay, Seven Mile has consistent swell and it's never overcrowded, but make sure you're there with friends as it's a looong beach.

Victoria

Lakes Entrance: This is a family-friendly spot that has fairly small beach breaks.

Torquay: Well known as one of Australia's homes of surfing (it's the home of Rip Curl and Quiksilver too), this has swells for all levels. Torquay itself is quite good but check with locals on the day. It can get cold in winter (10–12 degrees), so grab a wettie.

Sandy Point, Wilsons Promontory National Park: Consistent waves on this sandy beach break with little water movement and few rips.

Raffs, Apollo Bay: One of the safest beaches in the area with right-handers perfect for newbies.

Cat Bay, Phillip Island: Perfect for beginners with smaller, gentle waves.

South Australia

Baby Chinamans, Yorke Peninsula: A fairly slow left-hander, breaks up to 2 metres. Best at low tide.

The Dump, Dump Beach: Fun for beginners and kids and a good spot when other beaches in the area are too big.

Beach Breaks, Southport: Good in most conditions but watch for rips.

Moana Beach: South of the ramp is great for beginners. A family beach.

Sellicks Beach: Perfect for beginners as most experienced surfers stay away from this long sandy beach break.

Sellicks Beach

Western Australia

Ocean Beach, Denmark: A long break with easy, rolling waves and a handy rip to take you out the back (once you've mastered rips!).

Scarborough Beach, Perth: A super-popular beach with good surfing for all levels.

Lancelin Beach: North of Perth, Lancelin is great for beginners with gentle, rolling waves offering a long ride and a gorgeous clean ocean.

Back Beach: Just around the corner from Lancelin, this is also a good spot.

Madora Bay: Gentle beach break popular with surfers, body surfers and body boarders.

Mossies: A small right-hander with no dangers.

Ocean Beach

Tasmania

Carlton Beach: Waves are long and slow on this beach south of Hobart. Friendly people and good views.

Coles Beach, Devonport: Popular with locals, but watch the rocks.

Lauderdale Point, near Hobart: The smaller of point breaks in the area; excellent for longboards and fish boards.

Coles Bay: Hundreds of sand beach breaks to choose from with hardly anyone around. Great for paddling practise and amazing scenery.

Seven Mile Beach, near Hobart: A long right-hand break that can stretch for 200 metres over sand. Great scenery.

Cremorne Point: A perfect right-hander break over sand and rocks. Be careful at low tide or when it's really pumping.

South Clifton: Known as a great beginner, but can get a bit crowded over summer. But in Tasmania, that means about 10 people ... so anyone from a city will be fine.

Eaglehawk Neck Beach: Long punchy breaks over sand but does come with a steep takeoff.

Cloudy Beach, Neck Beach and Adventure Bay Beach, Bruny Island: Ranges from small beach breaks to massive swells so watch the winds.
A great day trip from Kettering.

Queensland

Noosa Main Beach: Mid-size waves off a sandy beach break. Great for attempting green waves in a friendly environment.

Worrim Beach, Bribie Island: Gorgeous scenery with gentle, rolling waves. Great for practising on green waves.

Coolum Beach, Sunshine Coast: Gentle waves and plenty of space. Voted the state's cleanest beach a couple of years back too.

Noosa

6.

Reso

People you need to know ...

Surfing Australia

www.surfingaustralia.com

Kingscliff NSW | (02) 6674 9888

Surfing Australia is the national governing body for surfing in Australia. They are recognised by the Australian Sports Commission, are a member of the International Surfing Association, and are a recognised federation of the Australian Olympic Committee. In short, these guys run surfing in Australia and make sure there is a pathway for beginner surfers like you and I to learn and advance in the sport, and potentially make it all the way to the pro tour. They do heaps of stuff, like run events and educational programs, provide accreditation for surf schools and look after national competitions and national competitors for all disciplines – longboards, shortboards and bodyboarding.

We're continually scouring the beaches for the next talent to go to greater heights. There is a pathway for everyone who wants to come surfing. **– Martin Grose, Surfing Australia.**

Surfing NSW

www.surfingnsw.com.au

South Maroubra | (02) 9349 7055

Surfing NSW was formed in 1963 and is the largest and longest running of the recognised state bodies for the sport of surfing in Australia. Supported by the NSW Department of Sport and Recreation, Surfing NSW strives to develop the sport of surfing so that it can reach its maximum potential through the organisation of professional events, coaching and educational programs. Surfing NSW is committed to developing future surfing stars. They are also passionate about safe surf lessons and support the state's 33 surf schools. They also run interesting surf events, so visit their website to keep updated about what's happening in the Surfing NSW camp.

Branches include:

- Newcastle Surfboard Association
- Northern Beaches Surfing Association
- NSW Bodyboarding Inc
- NSW Longboarding Association Inc
- Surfing Central Coast
- Surfing Far North Coast
- Surfing Illawarra Inc
- Surfing Mid North Coast Inc
- Surfing North Coast
- Surfing South Coast Inc
- Surfing Southside Inc
- Surfing Sutherland Shire

International Surfing Association

www.isasurf.org

California | (760) 931–0111

We're not sure why you'd want to contact these guys, but you definitely need to know they exist! The International Surfing Association is the world's governing body for surfing, bodyboarding and all waveriding activities. The ISA is a non-profit organisation that makes sure these sports continue to evolve worldwide by providing guidance and advice to its members on matters such as competition, judging, coaching, surf schools, anti-doping and drug testing.

Association of Surfing Professionals

www.aspworldtour.com

The ASP is the governing body of professional surfing across the globe, including the six professional circulates: the ASP World Tour, the ASP World Qualifying Series (WQS), the ASP World Longboard Tour (WLT), the ASP Pro Junior Series, the World Masters Championship and Specialty Events. The idea is to showcase the world's best in progressive formats and challenging locations. The ASP has an awesome website with interesting profiles on all pro surfers, so jump on and get the lowdown on what's happening worldwide.

Surf Life Saving Australia

www.slsa.com.au

Bondi | (02) 9300 4000

These are the guys and gals in red and who, steeped in Aussie tradition, patrol our beaches. They are also Australia's major water safety and rescue authority and one of the largest volunteer organisations in the country. They patrol 400 of the 11,560 beaches in Australia, while also training volunteer lifesavers and paid lifeguards to rescue people in need. They run school programs, provide helicopter, jet and offshore rescue boat services, and run our national Surf Life Saving Championships. Did you know ... there are 305 surf life saving clubs in Australia? These guys are great.

Surfrider Foundation Australia

www.surfrider.org.au

Coolangatta | (07) 5536 1021

Surfrider is a not-for-profit organisation that was formed to protect and maintain our enjoyment of Australia's gorgeous coast, coastal river catchments and offshore activities through conservation, advocacy, research and education. They are on the ground doing the hard yards for your benefit, so jump online and check them out. To whet your appetite, just last year, they stopped installation of parking meters along the Great Ocean Road, helped clean up remote marine debris in Tasmania and stopped the development of a cruise ship terminal on South Stradbroke Island which would have destroyed a main surf break. In short – these guys do some seriously good stuff for surfers!

SurfAid

www.surfaidinternational.org

North Sydney | (02) 9965 7325

SurfAid is one beautiful charity. Founded in Australia in 2004 by surfer and physician Dr Dave Jenkins, the idea was to help the people of the Mentawai Islands off the coast of Sumatra, Indonesia, who were suffering and in some cases, dying, from preventable diseases. SurfAid is dedicated to alleviating human suffering through community-based health programs. They are supported by the Australian and New Zealand governments, the global surfing community and the people of Mentawai.

The Disabled Surfers Association of Australia

www.disabledsurfers.org

PO Box 345, The Entrance NSW 2261

The DSA was established in 1986 by surfer Gary Blaschke who lost his kneecap in a motorcycle accident and subsequently underwent extensive rehabilitation. Through his loss, Gary realised there was a need to help surfers with disabilities get back into the water. The DSA runs a number of events and programs for surfers with disabilities to ensure they can get into the water and enjoy it with dignity.

Christian Surfers Australia

www.christiansurfers.org.au

Scarborough | 0419 935 536

Christian Surfers Australia are exactly what their name suggests – Christians who surf. They have been getting together for about 30 years and invite stand-up, bodyboarders, girls, mal riders, grommets, pro surfers, whatever, to join them. They run camps, day trips, comps and general get-togethers and also like to help their local communities while supporting those on the pro surfing scene with accommodation anywhere in Australia and chaplaincy in times of need.

Boardriding Clubs in NSW

A range of boardriding clubs exist – details of these can be found on the Surfing NSW website at **www.surfingnsw.com.au**.

Surf Schools in NSW

At the time of printing, there were 33 surf schools in NSW which were registered with Surfing Australia. Locations include ...

Arrawarra, Avoca Beach, Ballina/Evans Head, Bondi, Broulee, Byron Bay, Coffs Harbour, Crescent Head, Cronulla, Forster, Hallidays Point, Kingscliff, Manly, Maroubra, Nambucca Valley/South West Rocks, Newcastle, Old Bar, Port Macquarie, Port Stephens, Scotts Head, Soldiers Beach, Tathra Beach, Terrigal, Tweed Heads, Ulladulla, Umina, Wollongong, Yamba.

For full lists and contact details, visit the Surfing NSW website, **www.surfingnsw.com.au**.

Surf lingo

A-frame /ey-freym/ n.: A wave that resembles the letter 'A' because of its defined peak that simultaneously breaks to the left and right. Synonym: peak.

Aggro /ag-roh/ n.: Short for aggression in the water.

Bail /beyl/ n.: A parachuting term used to describe abandoning your board in a gnarly situation. You won't always have as 'easy' a landing as with skydiving … so look around you before you bail.

Bomb /bahm/ n.: The biggest wave or set of the day. Or what you may be doing a lot of while learning to surf.

Boost /boost/ v.: Any manoeuvre where a surfer (with his/her surfboard) leaves the face of the wave and flies through the air. Synonyms: air, aerial.

Blown out /blohn out/ v.: Surf destroyed or ruined by onshore wind. Also what happens when some surfers get creative on flat days and resort to alternative 'stimulation' via illicit herbaceous substances.

Caned /kand/ adj.: When a crucial wave slams you to the sea floor; an ugly wipeout. Synonyms: smoked, worked, smashed, nailed, hammered … and whatever other groovy slang for total annihilation you can conjure up.

Caught inside /kawt in-sahyd/ v.: Surfer trapped in the impact zone where the breaking waves give a good beating; usually happens after a wipeout or while paddling out.

Chinese wax job /chahy-neez waks job/ n.: Unwanted wax on the bottom of your board that has rubbed off the deck of a board placed on top of it.

Clubbies /kluhb-eez/ n.: Australian surf lifesavers.

Corduroy /kawr-duh-roi/ adj.: A solid swell with uniform lines resembling corduroy; many surfers' idea of Nirvana.

Ding /ding/ v. or n.: Damage on your board where the outer fibreglass skin has been damaged enough that the core foam is exposed. It happens to flesh occasionally as well so be careful out there.

Fakie /feyk-ee/ v.: To ride backwards (tail facing the beach) or switchfoot (with your opposite foot forward) on a surfboard.

Frothing /frawth-ing/ adj.: A state of such excitement that the mouth foams.

Grom /grom/ n.: Broadly used to describe a surfer who isn't old enough to drive, abbreviation for 'grommet'.

Hack /hak/ v.: A sharp change in direction; a synonym for surf. Hacked is also how you will feel after each surf during your prolonged learning curve.

Heavy /hev-ee/ adj.: Dangerous; serious. Also occasionally the type of friendly humanitarian you will meet at certain surf spots; smile kiddies!

Kook /kuk/ n.: A derogatory term for a beginner surfer; a difficult or obnoxious person. Interestingly, evidence suggests it derives from the ancient Hawaiian word kukai meaning ... well ... shit. Completely apt ... 'nough said.

Lineup /lahyn-uhp/ n.: Calm area beyond the break zone where a surfer waits to catch a wave. Alternatively, there is the police lineup, where offending snakes or drop-ins should be properly dealt with.

Lip /lip/ n.: Leading edge or rim of a wave. Also, what beginners or groms should never give to established locals.

Localism /lo'-ka-li-zum/ n.: A term designating the presence of occasionally threatening members from the area's surf community, usually protective and worthy of seniority, in the lineup.

Offshore /awf shohr/ n.: Wind that blows from land to the sea and creates the best conditions for tubes.

Onshore /awn shohr/ n.: Wind that blows from the ocean to land and provides the best conditions for aerials.

Pearling /purl-ing/ v.: The act of a surfboard piercing the water nose-first, causing the rider to plummet. Synonym: nose dive,

Quiver /kwiv-er/ n.: A surfer's collection of two or more surfboards. Alternatively, what you may do when faced with your first bad wipeout, first big wave or the realisation that the little kid paddling next to you is already way ahead of you in the style and performance stakes.

Rank /rangk/ adj.: Disgusting; bad; ugly; offensive.

Steamer /stee-mer/ n.: A full body wetsuit.

Thruster /thruhs-ter/ n.: Popular three-finned surfboard invented by Aussie Simon Anderson in 1980.

Trim /trim/ v.: Style of surfing when a surfer's speed allows them to maintain their position on the wave face without needing to generate speed from turns or manoeuvres. Especially important to good longboard surfing.

Wedge /wej/ n. or adj.: A very powerful A-frame wave formed when two waves combine after bouncing off an obstacle, such as a headland, jetty or break wall.

Wettie /wet-ee/ n.: A wetsuit.

Hanging at

BO

Welcome to Waverley!

We're lucky to boast three beautiful beaches – Bondi, Bronte and Tamarama – loved by millions of people from all walks of life.

Iconic Bondi Beach is recognised across the world and epitomises Australians' love for the beach and relaxed coastal lifestyle. It's arguably Australia's most popular beach, rating as Sydney's third top tourist destination and the unofficial surfing capital!

We have a long and proud surfing tradition at Bondi that's been established for more than a century. Surfing is a fun and exciting way to exercise. It's based on love for the ocean, respect for our environment and the thrill of catching the ultimate wave.

Bondi is a particularly great beach to surf because the conditions make it accessible pretty much every day of the year. At North Bondi, the small swells are great for beginners, while the southern end's conditions and larger swells are better suited for the more experienced surfers. Another advantage is that it isn't far from the hub of the city, so many urban dwellers can easily ride a wave before or after work or show off their manoeuvres over the weekend.

There are plenty of other things to do at Bondi and I encourage you to make the most of your time here. After your surf, why not check out an art exhibition at the Bondi Pavilion, grab a bite to eat at one of the many cafés and restaurants, or take look at the wide range of shops in the area. It truly lives up to its reputation as an international destination.

We hope you have a great time at our beautiful beach. Remember to have fun, be safe and always respect other swimmers and surfers, and help us keep our beach clean by following the simple rules and tips in this book. Enjoy your stay at Bondi!

Councillor Ingrid Strewe
Mayor, Waverley Council

Cr Strewe

Getting there

You can bus, train or car it to Bondi.

By train and bus:

- Take the train from Central Station to Bondi Junction, then head upstairs to the bus station and take the Bondi and Bay explorer bus to stop 11. Buses leave Bondi Junction every 10 minutes (and even more frequently in peak times), and every 15 minutes from 7.30 pm to midnight. They run hourly overnight.

By bus:

- Buses 380, 382 and 389 will also get you to Bondi. They all leave from Central Station.

- You can catch a limited-stops bus (bus 333) from Circular Quay in the city centre, which will take you straight to Bondi Beach (buy tickets from any CityRail station ticket office, or from Sydney Buses Transit Shop). Note: all buses to and from Bondi Beach go via Bondi Junction.

- You can also catch the Bondi Explorer bus which is popular with visitors. They leave every 30 minutes from Circular Quay for a 19-stop route through some of the most popular beaches around Bondi. You don't need to book, just jump on, pay the driver, and then you're free to get on and off all day at any of the 19 stops. What a ride!

For more information on buses, visit www.sydneybuses.info. For more information on trains, visit www.cityrail.info. For more information on Sydney ferries, visit www.sydneyferries.info. Or to speak with someone about all of these services, phone 13 15 00.

By foot:

- For those wanting to walk from Bondi Junction, it is roughly 2 km to the beach.

By car:

- There's a big push for people to leave their cars at home to keep us all carbon friendly – but also to help with parking, which can be a hassle in Bondi's crowded streets. However, if you're adamant you want to drive, it's about 30 minutes from the city centre. Head down Oxford St (which changes to Syd Enfield Drive and then Bondi Road) to bring you to the south entrance of Bondi Beach.

- There is paid parking in Bondi and, after a bit of hunting, you'll find a place to stop. Keep your meter full or your tickets renewed, or you will get a hefty fine.

- To grab a taxi, hail one from anywhere, or phone: RSL Cabs 13 15 81, Legion Cabs 13 14 51, Premier Cabs 13 10 17. For wheelchair-accessible cabs, call 1800 043 187.

Places to eat and drink

Bondi has so many places to eat you could spend your entire time hopping from place to place. You'll struggle to get really bad food here, with typically high standards from breakfast to dinner. There are cheap and cheerful haunts, but overall, Bondi boasts medium to pricey bites. No wonder, with real estate on the waterfront so pricey. For the same reason, restaurants on Campbell Parade tend to change hands regularly. Here are some favourites.

Sejuiced

Cafés

Speedo's Café (126 Ramsgate Ave): Up the northern end, Speedo's is a beachside café that leaves the frills at home. It's where the locals eat breakfast (which says something) because it's big and cheap for a café overlooking the water. It also has burgers, salads and good coffee. Speedo's supports local artists by showcasing local art. Open daily from 5.30 am until 6 pm. Brekky $6.50–$15.50, lunch $9.50–$17. Contact: (02) 9365 3622.

Australia's greatest
surf school
on Australia's
greatest beach!

128 Ramsgate Avenue, Bondi Beach NSW 2026
Phone: 61 2 9365 1800 Fax: 61 2 9365 1811 Email: info@letsgosurfing.com.au

letsgosurfing.com.au

Café Bondi (14 O'Brien St): Café Bondi is a bustling café a little away from the beach that buzzes with locals. Its food and service is consistently excellent, serving burgers and ribs through to salads, chicken, pasta and aged steaks. Head here to get away from the crowds of the beach in a simple, relaxed café. Pasta $13–$16, burgers $13–$17, steaks $20–$29, salads $10–$14. Open daily from 7 am to 10 pm. Contact: (02) 9300 6688.

Sejuiced (Shop 3, Queen Elizabeth Drv, The Pavilion): You can't go past this funky hole-in-the wall for a juice or snack beachside. Staff are great and pump juices and consistently-excellent coffee out all day long. They have all the other trimmings such as wheatgrass shots, power smoothies and healthy shakes plus brekky rolls and lurch wraps, and they even have roving sales teams on the beaches during peak summer periods. The 'morning glory' juice is a favourite, with orange, apple, mango, kiwifruit and ginkgo biloba and grapeseed booster which enhances libido (whatever turns you on!). Juices start from $4.40 and all wraps are $7.90. Open daily from 6:30 am to 3:30 pm in the winter and closing at 6 pm in summer. Contact: (02) 9300 0253.

Gusto Deli (2/16 Hall St): This place is considered to have some of the best coffee in the area. You can kick back with your morning coffee and friends in this legendary café where fabulous food and a warm atmosphere are the order of the day. Breakfast $10, lunch $12–$20. Open daily from 6.30 am to 6 pm. Contact: (02) 9130 4565.

Oporto (152 Campbell Pde): This local institution was founded in North Bondi in 1986 and quickly became a favourite amongst locals. Despite selling Portuguese-style chicken, Oporto is Aussie through and through (it's a 100 per cent Australian-owned company). This is the place to head for a quick refuelling after the beach or a late night. Burgers around $5. Open daily from 8 am to 11:30 pm. Contact: (02) 9130 8666.

Gertrude and Alice Café (46 Hall St): This quirky secondhand bookstore and café is a haven for the local arties. You definitely need to check out the relaxed ambience, great coffee, beautiful food and, of course, the books which lie around for café-goers to read! Café fare $5–$15. Open daily from 7:30 am till late. Contact: (02) 9130 5155.

AUSTRALIA'S LARGEST SURF SCHOOL NETWORK

Surfing Australia has more than 70 affiliated surf schools around Australia.

Surfing Australia's surf schools network delivers the Safe Surfing program, recognised by the Australian Sports Commission.

www.surfingaustralia.com

Trio Café (56 Campbell Parade): A more upmarket café that offers delicious (but a little more expensive) breakfasts and brunch. The menu is extensive and has a few different breakfast options like vanilla-infused couscous with goji berries served with a warm apple and pear compote and sweetened ricotta (what a mouthful) for $16. Plenty of shakes, juices and frappes are also on offer.
Breakfast $5–$19, brunch $14–$32. Open daily from 7.30 am to 3.30 pm. Contact: (02) 9365 6044.

Bondi Trattoria (34 Campbell Parade): Quality Italian and Australian flavours at reasonable prices. Try the chilli baked beans with fried polenta and parmesan ($9.50) for breakfast or the house-made rag pasta with duck and mushroom ragu ($18.90) for lunch. Breakfast $4–$16, lunch $14–$20, dinner $14–$30. Open Monday to Friday from 7 am till late and Saturday and Sunday from 8 am till late.
Contact: (02) 9365 4303.

Trio Café

Restaurants

Ravesi's (Cnr Campbell Parade and Hall St): An absolutely stunning restaurant overlooking the beach with a tapas-style menu that has expanded to pizza, pasta and seafood. A visit here is pure indulgence. Breakfast $12–$22, lunch and dinner $15–$35. Open Monday to Friday 12 noon to 3 pm and 6 pm to 10 pm, Saturday from 9 am to 4 pm and 6 pm to 10 pm, and Sunday 9 am to 4 pm only. Contact: (02) 9365 4422.

Ravesi's

Gelbison Pizzeria Ristorante Italiano (10 Lamrock Av): Quite the Bondi treasure, Gelbison has been serving scrumptious thin-crust pizza for years and the crowd is a real mixture of both local and visitors. Entrees $10, mains $20 and desserts are $8. BYO. Open daily from 5 pm until 10:30 pm. Contact: (02) 9130 4042.

Doughboy (290 Campbell Pde): Another good pizza joint serving authentic doughs up the northern end. Pizza $15–$24.50. Open daily from 5:30 pm until late. Contact: (02) 9365 5000.

SOUTH OF SYDNEY ON THE 13/7/07. – PHOTO: MARK NEWSHAM.

Hurricane's Grill and Bar Restaurant (130 Roscoe St): If you crave premium-quality Australian beef, tasty pork, lamb ribs and chicken in large quantities, then head here. Hurricane's signature dishes are marinated in special basting sauces originating from South Africa. Also on offer are burgers, fresh seafood, vegetarian dishes, salads. Mains $18–38. Open daily from 6 pm, and from 12 pm on Sundays. Contact: (02) 9130 7101.

Nina's Ploy Thai (132d Warners Ave): This is a small but charming place which produces fresh tasty Thai food. We recommend the boat noodle soup and the drunken noodles. Most dishes are around the $15 mark. Open Thursday to Tuesday from 12 noon until 10 pm. Contact (02) 9365 1118.

Big John's Pizza Café (199 Bondi Rd): Dining here is like eating with a traditional Italian family; think huge serves and food that is made with love. From fresh seafood to an extensive range of pizza and pasta dishes, this place will satisfy the healthiest of appetites. Pizza $10–18, mains $15. Open daily from 4.30 pm to 1 am. Contact: (02) 9369 1233.

Surfers helping surfers

The Disabled Surfers Association of Australia Inc. is a voluntary organisation giving anyone with a disability the opportunity for a safe and exciting surfing experience with trained supervisors. We hold "Hands-on Days" where both disabled and able bodied volunteers can join in and have a go. **Everyone is welcome.**

www.disabledsurfers.org

The fun, safe surfboard alternative for everyone

SOFTBOARDS AUSTRALIA has been producing boards since 1999, all constructed from A-grade polyethethylene with a high density slick bottom non rash decking material and soft fins.

Phone: (02) 9984 9710
Fax: (02) 9984 9702
Email: softba@bigpond.net.au
www.softboards.com.au

Flying Squirrel Tapas Parlour (249 Bondi Rd): At the time of writing, this was Bondi's new place to be seen, with morsels, martinis and music or in their words ... good eats and funky beats. A small, cozy and eccentric venue with a vibrant atmosphere and a fantastic modern tapas menu. Bookings for six or more are taken until 7 pm. Plates $5–$15. Open Monday to Saturday 6 pm to midnight and 5 pm to 10 pm on Sundays. Contact: (02) 9130 1033.

Thai Terrific (147 Curlewis St): Excellent modern Thai in a clean setting. Be sure to try house favourites the roasted duck pancake with cucumber ($12), or the crying tiger ($18), a tender yearling rump served with hot tamarind sauce on greens. Open Monday to Friday from 5 pm and Saturday and Sunday from noon. Soups $9–$15, curries $14–$19, whole fish $28. Contact: (02) 9365 7794.

Sean's Panaroma (270 Campbell Parade): A beautiful restaurant that's all about simplicity, serving up local produce and lots of seafood. The food is mouth-watering (it is considered one of Sydney's finest) from snapper to grass-fed scotch fillet and the décor is sophisticated yet homely. The menu sprawls on blackboards above the kitchen – but it is pricey. Pasta is around $25 (try the signature linguine) and mains are closer to $40. Dessert lovers should try the white chocolate nougat. Mains $16–$42. Open for lunch Friday to Sunday from noon, and dinner Wednesday to Saturday from 6 pm. Contact: (02) 9365 4924.

North Bondi Italian (118–120 Campbell Parade): With glass from top to bottom, this gorgeous restaurant sits at the northern end of Bondi. There's a posh crowd but the food is anything but pretentious. If you can afford it, you won't regret it. Pasta $25, mains $20–$35. Contact (02) 9300 4400.

Icebergs Dining Room and Bar (1 Notts Ave): This is a Bondi institution, perched over the ocean pool, on top of the Surf Life Saving Club and overlooking all of Bondi Beach through enormous glass windows. It's where you'll find the more-rich-and-famous-than-most, and comes with the price tag as well. The food (modern Mediterranean), the view, and the people all make for a gorgeous day or night out so if you can afford it, do it! Fully licensed (no BYO). Mains $38–$48 (and then there's the clay roasted whole suckling pig for $90 per person, although you'll need at least eight in your party). Open noon to midnight Tuesday to Saturday and noon to 10 pm on Sunday. Contact: (02) 9365 9000.

Pubs

Beach Road Hotel (71 Beach Rd): Fantastic pub in the thick of the activity, family-friendly yet great for backpackers, with budget meals on offer and lots of drinks specials. There's an outdoor area, live music and DJs, pool tables and a nice lounge area upstairs. Contact: (02) 9130 7247.

Hotel Bondi (178 Campbell Parade): Right across from the beach and with five bars, dance floor, beer garden, gaming room, a café, bistro and two bottle shops, you can't go past this haunt. It's clean, has friendly staff, and meals and drinks are well-priced. There's also live sport on the big screen in the Bombora Bar. Open daily from 6 pm to 10 pm. Contact: (02) 9130 3271.

Hotel Bondi

North Bondi RSL (118–120 Ramsgate Ave): This is a favourite with locals, with cheap beer, good pub food and fab views of the beach. You can easily kill a few hours – and a few rounds – here. Live music every Saturday. Open Monday from noon to 10 pm, Tuesday to Friday noon to 11 pm, Saturday 10 am to midnight and Sunday 10 am to 11 pm. Contact: (02) 9130 5152.

Robin Hood Hotel (cnr Carrington and Bronte roads, Waverley): The Robin Hood is everything you expect in an old-fashioned pub. It has plenty of locals who eye you on the way in, a low-key atmosphere and cheap drinks and food (yep, $6 steaks). But it's a nice place to sink down into and enjoy for a while, and it's away from the crowds. Open Monday to Saturday 10 am to 3 pm and until 10 pm on Sundays. Contact: (02) 9389 3477.

Cock 'n' Bull Hotel (89 Ebley St, Bondi Junction): An Irish-themed pub that is always busy with entertainment – typically on offer are cover bands midweek, a dance party on the weekends, and live Irish music on Monday nights. Décor is old-school. There are three bars, a gaming room, a TAB, a bistro serving up standard pub grub, and pool tables. Open 8 am to midnight Monday to Wednesday, 8 am to 2 am Thursday to Saturday, and 10 am to midnight on Sunday. Contact: (02) 9389 3004.

BONDI PAVILION
The centre of Bondi culture

Where entertainment, leisure and learning meet

Festivals, arts, performance, music, exhibitions, film, community and cultural events and activities

Queen Elizabeth Drive
Bondi Beach
Phone: 02 8362 3400
www.waverley.nsw.gov.au

Waverley
Council

Bars and Clubs

Drift at Ravesi's (118 Campbell Pde): This is Sydney's hottest beachside bar, boasting spectacular postcard views of Bondi Beach, an exquisite menu and a sophisticated cocktail and wine experience. Open Monday to Friday from 5 pm and from 3 pm on weekends. Contact: (02) 9365 4422.

Bondi Social (Level 1, 38 Campbell Pde): Bondi Social manages to combine a sense of downtown New York chic with the Bondi lifestyle. You can sit on the balcony and take in some of the best views of Bondi Beach going while sipping on a hip cocktail. This place manages to be both warm and intimate in winter and ooze beach sophistication in summer. Open from 6 pm Tuesday to Friday and from 12 noon on the weekends. Contact: (02) 9365 1788; www.bondisocial.com.au.

North Bondi RSL (118–120 Ramsgate Ave): Relax and enjoy the uninterrupted views of Bondi Beach from the wrap-around balcony and tuck into the tasty offerings from the club bistro. Open 12 noon till late Monday to Friday and from 10 am till late on the weekend. Contact: (02) 9130 3152; www.northbondirsl.com.au.

Bungabar (77 Hall St): With more than 50 cocktails to choose from, this laid-back bar is popular with locals and tourists. Open Monday to Friday from 4 pm to 11 pm and from 2 pm to 11 pm on Saturday and Sunday. Contact: (02) 9300 6766.

No Longer BB's Wine Bar (157 Curlewis St): This little wine bar has a cosy feel and a great wine list as well. A favourite with locals is the Guinness on tap for $5 a pint during the week. Check out the live folksy/blues acoustic music every night. Open daily from 3 pm until midnight. Contact: (02) 9365 3687.

Blue Chip Bar (Swiss Grand Hotel, cnr Campbell Pde and Beach Rd): This bar offers $3 pool daily and $10 meals every Monday night. There is live music every Saturday night and Sunday afternoon, trivia on Thursdays, DJs every Friday night, and $6 cocktails every Wednesday. Open until late every night. Contact: (02) 9365 5666.

Shopping

Bondi has an eclectic mix of shops, from the big surf gear stores through to boutique designer fashions. The best way to discover it is to spend a few hours wandering the streets, poking around to find the little nooks that house the best stuff. Campbell Parade has most of the surf gear, but head to Jacques Ave for a string of shops that are quintessentially Bondi.

Grandma Takes a Trip

Fashion

Bondi Surf Co. (Shop 2, 72–76 Campbell Pde): Your one-stop shop for all the biggest brands in surf wear, as well as a great range of products and accessories to help you hit the waves. Contact: (02) 9365 0870.

Mambo (80 Campbell Pde): This brand is 100 per cent Australian-owned and stocks surf wear and street wear for men, women and kids. The Bondi store stocks all the latest of the range and staff are friendly. Contact: (02) 9365 2255.

Bikini Island Boutique (Shop 1, 38-44 Campbell Pde): An institution since 1981, Bikini Island is your one stop shop for swimwear. With hundreds of styles to choose from, the helpful staff in this cute little shop opposite the beach are dedicated to helping find the bikini that suits you best. Contact: (02) 9300 9446.

From St Xavier (75a Gould St): This place embodies Bondi's laid back attitude while showcasing a mix of international and Australian fashion. This cutting-edge boutique stocks hip accessories and clothing from labels including Obey, Alice McCall and Sass & Bide. Contact: (02) 9365 4644.

Max's Shoes (150 Campbell Parade): A store that's been in Bondi for as long as most can remember, Max's has seen the place grow and change. Right on the beach and with great sales year-round, this shop draws people from all over Sydney for great shoes and boots. They are also known for their consistent sales. Contact: (02) 9300 9838.

Grandma Takes a Trip (79 Gould St): If you want to find a piece of vintage fashion from various decades, then head to this haven. Contact: (02) 9130 6262.

Tuchuzy (90 Gould St): This is the place for serious fashion lovers with some of the hottest trends and labels in women's, men's and children's clothing from Australia. Europe and the US. Contact: (02) 9365 5371.

Purdy Klampet (124a Roscoe St): A hip boutique for men and women who love to get the latest in fashion as well as more established brands such as State of Georgia and Saint Augustine Academy. Contact (02) 9300 8888.

Bowhouse (Shop 4/2a Jacques Ave): A pet store like no other, with a unique range of pet clothing, collars, weird and wacky accessories. Contact: (02) 9300 9390.

The Market Old and New Wares (2 Jacques Ave): Two gorgeous little shops with a large selection of furniture, knick-knacks and gifts. Come here if you want something special. Contact: (02) 9365 1315.

Abode (16a Hall St): For unique homewares and gifts, explore this quirky little store. You are guaranteed to find that special little something for any room in your house. You can find everything from books and beauty products to cooking utensils. Contact: (02) 9365 4706.

Silk Route (cnr Beach Rd and Gould St): The perfect place to find something for the person who has everything. Importing quality unique products from Morocco, India and Asia and stocking exclusively designed items that can be found nowhere else in Australia, Silk Route is a treasure-trove of products ranging from homewares to fashions and accessories. Contact: (02) 9365 0252.

Earthbound (9 Hall St): For soap, aromatic oils, incense, candles and other thoughtful gifts. Contact: (02) 9130 5069.

WADi Gallery (9 O'Brien St): This gallery has a combination of exhibitions from local artists, jewellery, gifts and a framing service. Contact: (02) 9365 6428.

Produce

The Earth Food Store (81 Gould St): Part supermarket, part café, The Earth Food Store is a one-stop health shop. The organic food and produce is just as delightful as the place itself (the owner used to run a theatre production company and this is evident in the store's set-up). Contact: (02) 9365 5098.

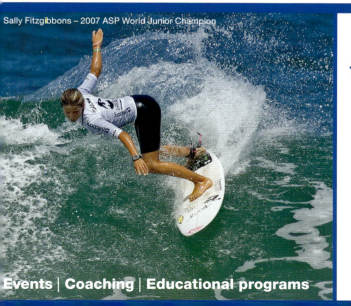

Sally Fitzgibbons – 2007 ASP World Junior Champion

Events | Coaching | Educational programs

Developing the sport of surfing in NSW to its maximum potential

SURFING NSW

Bondi Surf Seafoods (128 Campbell Pde): If you want fresh seafood, this is the place to get it. Bondi Surf Seafoods is one of the oldest and liveliest fish shops in Bondi and they stock fresh fish daily from the Sydney Fish markets. Open daily. Contact: (02) 9130 4554.

Fleur de Lys Patisserie (Shop 1, 148 Curlewis St): Mouth-watering pastries, tarts, cakes, biscuits and slices, all baked daily at this gorgeous little place. Contact: (02) 9365 4834.

Services

Banks and ATMs: Commonwealth Bank, 31 Hall St, contact: (02) 9130 5247. ANZ, 11 Hall St, contact: (02) 9365 3072. St George, 186 Campbell Parade (through Bondi Beach Convenience, no late access), contact: 13 33 30.

Money exchange: International Currency Services Australia, Shop 2/178 Campbell Parade, contact: (02) 9365 3876. Currency Exchange International, 164 Campbell Parade, contact: (02) 9300 8484.

Bondi lifeguard

Petrol: Caltex, 321 Old South Head Rd, contact: (02) 9130 3082. Caltex, 51 Bondi Rd, contact: (02) 9387 8750.

Police: 77 Gould St, contact: (02) 9365 9699.

Bondi Fire Station: Old South Head and Gilgandra Roads, contact: (02) 9300 9370.

State Emergency Service: 13 25 00.

Waverley Council: Cnr Paul St and Bondi Rd, Bondi Junction, contact: (02) 9369 8000.

Bondi Lifeguard Tower: Bondi Beach, contact: (02) 8362 3450.

Surf clubs: Bondi Surf Bathers' Life Saving Club, Queen Elizabeth Drv, contact: (02) 9300 9279.

Newsagents: Ben Buckler Newsagency, 35 Campbell Parade, contact: (02) 9130 2774. Bondi Centre Newsagency, 161 Bondi Rd, contact: (02) 9387 1087. Six Ways Newsagency, 64–66 Hall St, contact: (02) 9365 5576. Sevenways Newsagency, Shop 2, 60 Blair St, North Bondi, contact: (02) 9130 7372. Bondi Beach Newsagent, 13a Campbell Parade, contact: (02) 9130 4557. Bondi Rd Newsagency, 261 Bondi Rd, contact: (02) 9130 5428.

Hospitals and medical: Bondi Road Medical Centre, 248 Bondi Rd, contact: (02) 9389 8000. Bondi Family Health Care, 260a Bondi Rd, contact: (02) 9365 1333. Bondi Junction Private Hospital, 21 Spring Rd, contact: (02) 9387 6622. Bondi Family Medical Practice, 194 Bondi Rd, contact: (02) 9389 8000. Bondi Rd Family Medical Practice, 9 Bondi Rd, contact: (02) 9389 4333. Brighton Boulevard Medical Practice, 99 Brighton Boulevard, contact: (02) 9130 1247. Castlefield Family Practice, 1a Castlefield St, contact: (02) 9130 5994.

Chemist: Bondi Day and Night Pharmacy, 132 Campbell Parade, contact: (02) 9130 2361. Arkle Pharmacy, 81 Bondi Rd, contact: (02) 9389 3118. Bondi Centre Pharmacy, 146 Campbell Pde, contact: (02) 9130 8446. Pharmacy at Bondi, 81 Hall St, contact: (02) 9130 4680. Glenayr Pharmacy, 114 Glenayr Ave, contact: (02) 9130 1328. Basger's Pharmacy, Murriverie Rd, North Bondi, contact: (02) 9130 7515.

Convenience stories: 7-Eleven, 15 Hall St, contact: (02) 9130 5037. The Oz 5 Convenience Store, 19–23 O'Brien St, contact: (02) 9130 8578. Ocean Convenience Store, 152 Campbell Pde, contact: (02) 9130 2171. Bondi Convenience Store, 22 Campbell Pde, contact: (02) 9130 8322.

Public phones: Located at 45 Campbell Parade and 80 Brighton Boulevard.

Internet: Phone Net Café, 73–75 Hall St, contact: (02) 9365 0681. Mailbox Internet Café, Shop 3a, 34 Campbell Pde, contact: (02) 9300 0318. Global Gossip Bondi Beach, 37 Hall St, contact: (02) 9365 4811. Surfnet Internet Café, 54 Spring St, Bondi Junction, contact: (02) 9386 4066.

Post Office: Bondi Beach Licensed Post Office, 20 Hall St, contact: 13 13 18. Bondi Licensed Post Office, 127 Bondi Rd, contact: 13 13 18.

Transport and taxis: Taxis Combined, contact: 13 33 00. Legion Cabs, contact: 13 14 51. Sydney Buses, contact: 13 15 00. Bondi Junction train station, Grafton St, Bondi Junction, contact: (02) 9379 4023.

Bondi Taxis

Car hire: Discount Car and Truck Rentals, 204 Oxford St, Bondi Junction, contact: (02) 9389 7377.

Churches: Church at the Beach Bondi (Bondi Christian Life Centre), Unit 11, 184–186 Campbell Pde, contact: (02) 9130 1299. St Patrick's Church, 2 Wellington St, contact: (02) 9365 1195. St Andrew's Anglican Church, 60 Wairoa Av, contact: (02) 9130 1211. St Anne's Catholic Church, cnr Mitchell and Oakley sts, contact: (02) 9130 7225. Uniting Church of Australia, contact: (02) 9130 3445. Sisters of St Joseph, 4 Wellington St, contact: (02) 9130 6804.

Cinemas: Greater Union Cinema, Level 7, 500 Oxford St, Bondi Junction, contact: (02) 9300 1555.

Alcohol-free zones

Bondi Beach has an alcohol-free zone in public places, stretching from Hunter Park in the south to Ray O'Keefe Reserve up north, which covers the entire beach front and the Pavilion. It also stretches inland to Blair St, so keep off the grog at the beach or the park or on any of the streets in the outlined area. Head to the pubs, clubs and restaurants for a top-up if need be!

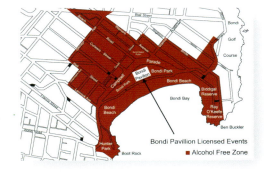

Places to stay

There is a large range of accommodation in Bondi, with plenty on the waterfront. Prices can be high but there's a good range of backpacker accommodation down at the southern end. For places that are cheaper still, head inland – going north or south won't help your cause a great deal.

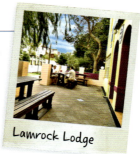
Lamrock Lodge

Noah's Backpackers (2 Campbell Pde): Noah's is well known to locals and travellers for some of the cheapest beds in Bondi. It's right across the road from the beach and reception staff are fluent in Japanese, Hebrew and Swedish. Prices start at $20 per person per night (share rooms only) and $50 per person per night for a single room. Contact: (02) 9365 7100; www.noahsbondibeach.com.

Lamrock Lodge (19 Lamrock Ave): Affordable beachside digs with four-bed dorms from $23 per person. Twin or double rooms $49 per person per night and single rooms from $35. Contact: (02) 9130 5063; www.lamrocklodge.com.

Bondi Serviced Apartments (212 Bondi Rd): About 900 m from the beach and 100 m from Bondi Junction. Offers budget and standard apartment accommodation from $85 in winter and $105 in summer. Contact: (02) 8837 8000; www.bondi-serviced-apartments.com.au.

Surfside Backpackers (35a Hall St): Clean, budget accommodation with dorm beds from $21 per night and double/twins from $55 per night. Contact: (02) 9365 4900; www.surfsidebackpackers.com.au.

The Bondi Sands (252 Campbell Parade): Just 60 m from the sand, this clean and cheap joint is a great accommodation option. Offers dorm rooms (includes female only) as well as double, twin and triple options, and has a rooftop deck that overlooks the beach and Campbell Parade. Dorms from $28 per person and doubles $80. Contact: (02) 9365 4900.

Bondi Beach Guest House (28 Sir Thomas Mitchell Rd): About 100 m from the beach, this is an elegant guesthouse set amongst trees and gardens. Includes outdoor entertaining and sunning areas perfect for a relaxing stay by the water. Rooms from $95 single and $135 double, ensuite rooms $225 per night. Contact: (02) 9300 0369; www.bondibeachhouse.com.au.

Swiss Grand Resort and Spa (cnr Campbell Pde and Beach Rd): Luxurious accommodation right on the beach. Amazing views, two restaurants, three bars, health club and gym, heated swimming pool, day spa and jacuzzi. Prices from $580 to $1265. Contact: (02) 9365 5666; www.swissgrand.com.au.

Ravesi's (118 Campbell Pde): Houses 12 stunning and unique designer guest rooms created by renowned designer and abstract artist Dane van Bree. Ravesi's offers understated luxury and a fabulous location just opposite the beach. Rooms from $240 to $495 per single/double room per night. Contact (02) 9365 4422; www.ravesis.com.au.

SurfAid ambassador and two-time world surfing champion Tom Carroll and his daughter Mimi with Mentawai children. Photo: Kirk Willcox/SAI

SurfAid International
A non-profit humanitarian organisation improving the health and wellbeing of people living in isolated surfing regions.
www.surfaidinternational.org

Things to do

Bondi is about sun, sand, surf and food so the best way to enjoy it is to wander the streets, laze on the beach and eat out – as often as you can. Here's the run down on a few activities you can (or must) do. There is unfortunately no dedicated visitor information centre in town, but most accommodation spots have extensive lists on seasonal activities on offer.

Bondi Skate Park

Have a surf: Okay, so this is on the top of the list for a reason. Reading this book, you just can't escape it, and with such a beautiful beach before you, there's always something to ride for newbie surfers like yourself. Take a lesson with the guys at Lets Go Surfing Bondi who operate 365 days of the year and are the only licensed surf school on the beach. They also have a retail store stocking all things surf at 128 Ramsgate Ave, just across the road from the kids' pool at North Bondi. Contact: (02) 9365 1800; www.letsgosurfing.com.au.

Visit the markets: For almost 20 years, the Bondi Beach Market has been providing locals and tourists with gear by up-and-coming designers, handmade jewellery, homewares, secondhand clothes and retro furniture. Held every Sunday from 10 am to 5 pm at the Bondi Beach Public School (for more details on the markets, see the end of this section).

Walk from Bondi to Coogee: People from all over the world come to walk this 6 km stretch of coastline that passes by some of Sydney's best beaches. The trail starts at Icebergs and takes you up to Mackenzie's Point, on to Tamarama, Bronte, and Clovelly, ending up at Coogee Beach. A portion of this walk, from Bondi to Bronte, houses the famous Sculpture by the Sea exhibition each year (see below for more details). This section of the walk is 3.4 km. For a self-guided tour, visit www.selfguidedwalkingtours.com where you can download a commentary for your iPod or MP3 player for just $10.

Take in some culture at The Pavilion: The Bondi Pavilion, right in the centre on the beach, has been Bondi's cultural hub since 1928. It originally housed the Turkish Baths but now hosts annual events from the South American Festival to Carols by the Sea and the Bondi Waves music workshops. Sign up for music, art or meditation classes to name a few or see a local art exhibition or play. Find out what is happening in Bondi on the noticeboards. There is always something happening at the Bondi Pavilion, which is located on Queen Elizabeth Drive, Bondi Beach. Contact: (02) 8362 3400; www.waverley.nsw.gov.au/info/pavilion.

People-watch by the Pavilion: Bondi has often been referred to as 'the people's beach' and it's no wonder. With thousands of people passing by every day, there are hours to be spent observing the diverse crowd from the busloads that arrive just to touch the sand to the surf school lessons, the personal training sessions and the local clubs doing ocean swims. Grab a juice or ice cream, sit yourself down and let the day – and the people – pass you by.

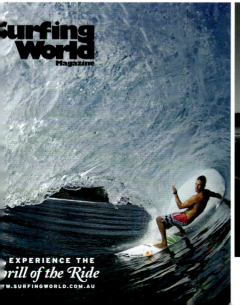

Swim at Icebergs: Yes there is the beach, but Icebergs is steeped in history where every winter up to 700 people jump into freezing water for charity. It started in 1929 when a group of guys met there every Sunday to race in freezing water. Today the site is a three-storey venue from pool to restaurant and it also houses the Bondi Icebergs Swimming Club. Swim any time of the week ($4.50 adults, $2.50 children) or watch morning races ($1) every morning from the first weekend in May until the last weekend in September. Contact: (02) 9130 4804; www.icebergs.com.au.

Barbecue at North Bondi: Kick back and enjoy snags and a couple of drinks with friends at Biddigal Park on Ramsgate Ave, the only park right on the beach with barbecues installed. There are four coin-operated barbecues (20¢) on site which all operate until dusk. The grassy area overlooks the pool and beach, and has plenty of shade and play areas.

Bondi Baths

Surfrider Foundation®

Surfrider Foundation Australia is a not-for-profit organisation dedicated to protecting Australia's oceans, waves and beaches through conservation, activism, research and education.

Catch the wave.

www.surfrider.org.au

Visit the Organic Food Market (Bondi Junction/Bondi Mall): Bondi residents are notorious for their healthy and active lifestyles so when in Rome ... The Organic Food Market is on every Thursday to Sunday with fresh meat, seafood, cheese, vegetables, fruit and hot snacks. Open 9 am to 5 pm on Thursdays and Fridays. On the weekend the market moves to the BJ Bazaar in the Oxford St Mall, Bondi Junction, and is open Saturday and Sundays, 10 am to 5 pm.

Take the Bondi Explorer: A bus that travels the streets of Bondi giving tourists a perfect view of all things Bondi. There are 19 stops taking in Bondi, Tamarama, Bronte and Coogee. Travellers can get on and off whenever they please, with the service running all day and tickets purchased in 24-hour blocks. Tickets $39 adult, $19 children, $97 family. Contact: (02) 13 15 00; www.sydneypass.info/bondiexplorer. Timetables from www.131500.info.

Take a yoga class: If you take an early morning walk, you'll see yoga enthusiasts doing their thing on Bondi Beach or in the adjacent parklands. For those wanting a class Dharma Shala Yoga (108 Brighton Boulevard) is a local haunt that has become rather iconic in yoga circles. They specialise in Vinyasa variations of Hatha yoga, with staff experienced in western and Indian ashram traditions. Casual classes are $17 and private classes are available. Contact: (02) 9365 5033.

Surf on land at the Bondi Skate Park: Right beside the beach, locals spend hours at this place, especially when the surf is flat. It's free to skate – but even if you aren't willing to brave the pain of the concrete falls, you can just sit back and watch.

Play golf by the sea: Right by the North Bondi cliffs is Bondi Golf Course (5 Military Rd), a great way to kill a few hours in the sea breeze under the Bondi sun. It's an old-style links course and it's open to the public daily until dark (check the website for competition times). Prices are $20 for 18 holes, $15 for 9 holes, students and pensioners $15, cart $25–$35, set hire $20. Contact: (02) 9130 1981; www.bondigolf.com.au.

Walk to Ben Buckler: Ben Buckler is the headland at North Bondi which gets great views of the beach, the coast and the pounding surf. There is a big rock, fittingly called 'Big Rock', a 235-tonne boulder which is believed to have been thrown up there by heavy seas on 15 July 1912. It's worth a visit, especially when the surf is roaring.

Local markets

Bondi boasts one main regular market, and it's worth checking out.

Where? On the beachfront grounds of Bondi Beach Public School, Campbell Parade.

When? Every Sunday from 10 am to 5 pm.

Getting there: The Bondi markets are located right across the road from Bondi Beach. You can't miss them.

What to expect: If you want to discover the next big thing in Australian fashion, then head to the Bondi markets. Local designer brands such as Sass & Bide began selling their clothing here before they made it big. There is something to satisfy everyone, from exotic imports, handmade jewellery, arts, crafts, homewares, retro furniture and vintage clothes.

Bondi Markets

More info: www.bondimarkets.com.au.

Annual events

There is a range of festivals and events based in Bondi on offer throughout the year:

Roughwater Swim: Held for more than 15 years, more than 650 swimmers take part in this 2 km annual ocean swim. It has attracted Olympians such as Murray Rose, John Konrads, Neil Rogers, Hayley Lewis and Malcolm Allen. The race starts at 10 am at North Bondi on the second Sunday in January.

Flickerfest: The academy-accredited short film festival Flickerfest screens short films from Australia and around the world. It's usually held in early January, and movies are screened under the stars in a relaxed environment. It then tours to 17 other venues across Australia.

North Bondi Classic: Held on the first Sunday in February, this is a 2 km, two-swim event where 1000 swimmers hit the water at Bondi.

South American Festival: A celebration of all things South American: dance, food and culture. It's held on the third Sunday in February.

Sun-Herald City to Surf: A 14 km race from Sydney Town Hall in the CBD to Bondi, the City to Surf attracts 60,000 runners every year and ends with a spectacle on Bondi Beach. Race starts 9 am and is held on the second Sunday in August.

Festival of the Winds: An internationally acclaimed kite festival that brings the beach to life with colour on the second Sunday in September. A great day for kids – old and young.

Sculpture by the Sea: Late October/every November, more than 100 sculptures from around the world are placed on the clifftop walk from Bondi to Tamarama, creating Australia's largest annual outdoor art exhibition – and it's free. An eclectic mix of art that draws more than 500,000 every year. Contact: (02) 8399 0233; www.sculpturebythesea.com.

Bondi to Bronte Ocean Swim: A 2.5 km race held on the first Sunday in December that's famous with locals and elite swimmers.

Christmas/New Year celebrations: Held between December 25 and January 1. There's always a huge line-up of events from live bands to fireworks.

Beyond Bondi

Several excellent beaches border the Bondi neighbourhood, each with their own little personality. Hopping between them all can be an interesting and relaxing day out.

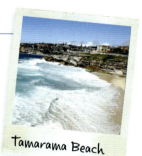

Tamarama Beach

Tamarama

A small beach in a swanky suburb with a groovy beachside café. There's often a beach volleyball net set up and a line-up of competitors waiting to challenge. Make sure you take care in the surf here, as it can get a little boisterous. Because the beach is so small and there are point breaks on both sides, there are often strong rips and currents behind this beautiful oasis. You'll see plenty of surfers despite the small surf zone, with swells reaching up to 4.5 m. The beach is patrolled by the Tamarama Surf Life Saving Club which has not had a swimmer die under its care in 100 years (nice record, guys!).

European settlers ignored the Aboriginal name for the area – 'Gamma Gamma' – during the eighteenth century, choosing instead to call the beach Dixon Bay. But in the 1800s, the beach was officially dubbed Tamarama after the area's original Aboriginal nomenclature. Locals call it Tama or 'Glamarama' because of the crowd it attracts (yep, the movie stars and rich and famous like this little place).

Getting there: Either walk from Bondi (15 minutes) or take bus 361 from Central Station or Bondi Junction.

Bronte

Just south of Tamarama you'll come across a picturesque valley that is home to Bronte Beach. Juxtaposed against the notoriously rough surf and beautiful sand is a large grassy knoll that gets jam-packed in the summertime, with people lounging from early till late, eating, playing and watching.

Bronte is an easygoing beach and is popular with families. It has an excellent café strip with cheap eats like fish burgers for $5 through to gourmet mains at $35 a pop. There are also prepaid barbecues on the grass which require a handful of 20¢ pieces.

The main beach can produce fairly powerful surf, so swimmers need to be mindful. It's home to The Bronte Express, a famous rip by the south headland which has been known to take swimmers out to sea.

For experienced swimmers or surfers, the south headland is a great entry point to the line-up. If you're inexperienced or can't be bothered dodging the waves on the day, there is also an ocean pool and what locals call the 'boogie hole' which is a little swimming hole between the main beach and ocean pool sheltered from the swell which offers a heap of fun without the fuss. Bronte is patrolled by the Bronte Life Saving Club – so look for the flags and you'll be fine.

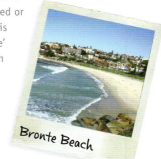

Bronte Beach

Getting there: A walk from Bondi to Bronte takes about 30 minutes or you can grab bus 378 from Central Station, Bondi Junction or Bondi.

Clovelly

Clovelly is a small protected beach in a narrow bay that doesn't get any surf. It was known as Little Coogee until 1913, and is popular with families, inexperienced swimmers or those who just want to play without the fuss of waves. If you can source a snorkel and goggles, the calm waters make for a great arvo out. Clovelly Hotel is a great place to wash down an ale after a day in the hot sun.

Getting there: A walk from Bondi takes about 40 minutes or grab the 339 bus from the QVB bus station in the city, just behind the Queen Victoria Building.

Coogee

Coogee is a spacious beach with parklands, barbecues and cafés, making it a popular place for bigger groups. It is known for attracting backpackers and a younger crowd. That being said, because of its size, there is room for everyone, from big family groups to the cosy couple looking for their own piece of sand to get away from it all.

Coogee

Getting there: Buses 372, 373 and 374 will get you there from the city or Central Station. From Bondi Junction, grab bus 353 which goes via Eastgardens shopping centre.

Bondi Junction

Bondi Junction is the commercial hub of the city's eastern suburbs. It houses one of the main train terminuses (Eastern Suburbs line) as well as quite a large bus depot. But while it's commercial it's certainly not ugly.

Bondi Junction has a large and relatively new shopping centre which has become a premier shopping destination with everyday wear through to designer labels. The outdoor mall area is fun to browse for a bargain and there's a food and produce market in the mall each Saturday and Sunday. Head to Bondi Junction for shopping, movies or for a city feel within a city. It's also the main transport hub for trains and buses at this end of town.

Dudley Page Reserve

This is a small reserve on Military Rd, Dover Heights, but one that packs a punch. It has fantastic views over the city of Sydney (some say the best), showcasing the Opera House, Harbour Bridge and Centrepoint Tower. The reserve is a popular spot with locals to watch the famous Sydney Harbour fireworks display on New Year's Eve. If you're around at this time, get there early to nab your spot, as like any location on the harbour, it'll fill up fast!

Useful websites

www gobondi.com

www bondimarkets.com.au

www bondifm.com.au

www cyberbondi.com.au

www bondivillage.com

www waverley.nsw.gov.au

www bondisurfclub.com

www northbondisurfclub.com

www tamaramaslsc.org

A quick chat ...

with local actor GYTON GRANTLEY about life in Bondi

Actor Gyton Grantley says he wouldn't live anywhere else, having moved from Brisbane to North Bondi a few years ago. The laid-back *Underbelly* actor lives 30 seconds from the waves and says he's on the sand every day without fail. We talked about life in Bondi ... over a sandcastle-making session!

Love about Bondi: The beach! Look at this place, it's beautiful. I tell my friends that I don't actually live in Sydney, but this small coastal town called North Bondi. It's like a bubble, you come here and don't leave because you have everything here ... groceries, dry cleaning and banking, and most of my friends live here too. And where else can you wake up and be in the water in 30 seconds? I'm here every day, without fail.

The beach: You can surf, fish, snorkel, walk, run, lie here, make sandcastles, it's just too good. In summer we have been known to bring my table tennis table down here and put it in kiddies' corner. It fits perfectly at high tide, the table is about 15 cm out of the water.

Beach culture: Bondi is the epicentre of the beach culture in Sydney, I think. The northern beaches are beautiful and have heaps better surf for sure, but Bondi is where it's happening.

Swim and surf: I surf in the south and swim up north. I go snorkelling off the point and fishing below the golf course. There's a little secret pathway down there and you can climb the cliff face. Good luck trying to find it!

Surfing: I've only been surfing for four years and I wouldn't even say that I'm very good but I do love it. Bondi is great for beginners because there are so many people learning to surf all the time and there are nice soft foamies that you can jump on.

Advice for beginners: Stay out of the way!

Eat: I like Oporto, everyone does. Nina's Ploy is always good for Thai as well.

A quick word ...

Bondi lads Marco, Chad and Wes are taking their catchy groove-rock music to the world. A self-confessed activist band, they are passionate about preserving nature and bringing people together. Formerly known as Jada, they are now Mojada or 'more Jada' and have recently shared the stage with the likes of Thirsty Merc, Pete Murray, Ozomatli and The Beautiful Girls. Fresh from a trip to the US, we caught up with them at North Bondi.

Mojada: We're a couple of guys with guitars singing our hearts out, that's all! We started writing music together about seven years ago here in Bondi. People have come and gone, a lot of songs have come and gone.

More than music: We are really an activist band when it comes down to it. We did a big anti-whaling event here in Bondi and it was great to see the local surfing community and artistic community come out and support a good cause. We joined up with Bunna from the band Coloured Stone – he's played with the likes of Yothu Yindi. The whaling issue is a window to greater problems, for example there's a hundred million sharks being taken out of the sea every year for their fins. This event was our first big step and we plan to do a lot more from here on. We want to be involved in protecting the earth and its inhabitants.

Bondi loves: The beach is it really, being able to chill out and hang out on the beach, even in winter. You can't do that in many places around the world. The waves are pretty good around here and there's a great community that's really artistic.

"We are really an activist band when it comes down to it."

with Bondi-based band MOJADA

"The music culture in Bondi is excellent. It's great to see a good live music culture and that's important ..."

Music culture: The music culture in Bondi is excellent. It's great to see a good live music culture and that's important because a lot of us grew up on that [playing gigs], it's what improved our musical skills and what will improve other people's musical skills. That's how you learn as a musician. The North Bondi RSL is a big supporter of live music. A lot of places are just content to throw a DJ on ... really it's their loss.

Our music: We've got elements of funk, pop, reggae, rock. We try to make our music uplifting, pretty positive stuff that's good to dance to. We hit the road as an unknown band back in the beginning and found that if we wanted to get people up out of their chairs in venues around the country, we had to get moving and make high energy funk and rock. We have this saying 'monkey's on your back' and that means a song is groovin'.

Drink: North Bondi RSL for really cheap drinks, great food and live music, and Bunga Bar is an old favourite.

Eat: Skinny Dip, Gertrude and Alice, Beach Burrito, Rice Pot, Le Paris Go, Green's Café for breakfast, and Beach Road for a schnitzel and spaghetti.

Visitor musts: Go surfing (don't drop in on the locals!), the Bondi to Bronte walk, do a few bombs off the rocks up north, walk the beach ... just get out in the fresh air as much as you can.

Acknowle

In the short time (five months) it took us to create and produce these books, we have just had such extraordinary people supporting us along the way ... amazing surfers, business people, friends and creatives – thank you – we really do feel part of a much greater community now and look forward to many more shared journeys and happy memories together.

dgements

Mel Carswell: My fellow dreamer and doer and the most amazing, loyal, passionate person I have ever had the pleasure of working with. You take my crazy over the top ideas and work your guts out to help me make them a reality. Without your tenacity, unbelievable writing skills, patience and belief in our vision, these books would never have happened. Here's to many more years of creating big visions, amazing products and traversing the world together.

Barton Lynch: One of the most humble, hilarious and talented people we know – we just LOVE you! Thanks for your belief in this project and just jumping in all over the place and helping us on so many levels. You are truly a legend!

Thanks also to our new surfing buddies: Martin Grose, Mark Windon, Ben Whibley, Merrilee Barnes, Brenda Miley, Craig Wachholz, Serena and Matt Adams, Matt Grainger.

All those amazing surfers we take so much inspiration from.

Our wonderful partners as listed in the supporters page.

Other people we just love: Eugene Tan (Aquabumps), Jenni Burgess (Manly Chamber), Meegan Clancy (Manly Mainstreet), Stephen Lucas (Bondi Chamber), Russell Mills (Northern Rivers Tourism), Rusty Miller, Chris Tola (Surfrider), Andrew McEvoy (Tourism SA), Damian Ward (HWL Lawyers), Grant Mapas (Cancer Council), Mayor Ingrid Strewe (Waverley Council), Mayor Jan Barham (Byron Council), Mayor Peter Macdonald (Manly Council), Andy Ruwald (Sejuiced), Denver Beven, Mark Eymes (Billabong, Surfer HQ), Gary James (Surfer HQ), Box Kerr (Bondi Rescue), Derek Recio (Waves and Tracks), Marine Carollo (Rip Curl), Dave Jenkins (Surf Aid International), Tony Eldridge, Rebecca Olive, Doug Lees (Surfing World), Brad Morgan and Brad Malyon (Frothers), Kim Sundell (Coastalwatch), Ben Kirkwood (Byron Beach Café), Danny Wills, Dayyan Neve, Kieren Perrow, Layne Beachley, Steph Gilmore, Mick Fanning, Midget Farrelly, Sally Fitzgibbon, Perth Standlick, Pam Burridge, Rusty Miller, Marco, Chad and Wes of Mojada, Gyton Grantley, Big Wave Dave.

The extended Messenger team: Mel Carswell, Caroline Butterworth, Andrea Woodman, Emma Cooney, Heidi Helyard, Anna Crago, Sarah Christensen, Jeremy Stevens, Julia Van Horn, Claire Livingston, Theo Chan, Nathan Hill, Andrew McIntosh.

And of course, the cheerleading squad: David Price, Dan Martin, Andrew Lemon, Andrew Carswell, Kate Messenger, Sally Muller, Bobbi McIlwraith, Ed Petrie.

These books really have just been such an exciting journey and proof that with a great team of supporters, anything is truly possible! We look forward to doing it all again shortly.

Sponsor's

gallery

Industry Partners

Surf School Partners

Council and Business Partners

Tourism Partners

Other Surfing Partners

Business Partners

Media Partners

Photography Partners

Sarah C Photography

OCEAN PHOTOGRAPHY
www.oceanphotography.com.au

Charity/Not for Profit Partners

The Messenger Group

The Messenger Group is a collaboration of a number of creative companies specialising in innovative out of the box, lateral publishing solutions. We have never been limited, locked into or entrenched in any way by conventions and traditional approaches. We love to push comfort zones and invoke attitudinal shifts to make extraordinary things happen.

Our services include:

- Dynamic, progressive, creative book production including project management, ghost writing, editing, proofing, photography, print

- Design and print of marketing collateral including business cards, letterhead, banners, postcards, posters, bookmarks

- Marketing, funding and distribution strategies

- Print brokerage for corporate brochures and books

Our mission is to make the dreams of our clients come alive. We are passionate about having fun and letting our imaginations soar beyond predictable solutions, demonstrating that there is always more than one way to do anything.

With the *Learn to Surf* series, Messenger Publishing hopes to create a vibrant tool for local communities and visitors alike. We love Australia and the outdoors, we love our hot tourism spots, we love our people and we're proud to produce a series of books that reflects just that. Thank you for walking this journey with us.

www.messengerpublishing.com.au

messenger

Photo credits

All photography remains the copyright of the individual photographers, including:

ii: Leigh Warner
vii: Sarah C Photography
viii, xi: Sarah C Photography
xii: Douglas H Kim Photography
xiii: Anke Van Wyk
xvi: Videowokart
xvii: Sarah C Photography
xviii: Serious Guy
1: Daniel Krzowski
2: Top L-R: Waverley Council, Waverley Council, Waverley Council, Waverley Council, Carly Reeves, Waverley Council. Bottom L-R: Waverley Council, Waverley Council, Waverley Council, Waverley Council, Waverley Council, Jamalludin Bin Abu Seman Din.
4: Leigh Warner
5: Jan Rysavy
6: Sarah C Photography
7: Top L-R: Benton Duthie, Bondi Council. Middle L-R: Jeremy Edwards, Benton Duthie. Bottom L-R: David Combes, Celso Dinz.
10: Waverley Council
12: Feng Yu
13: Top L-R: Sarah C Photography, David Combes. Middle L-R: Waverley Council, Waverley Council, Sarah C Photography. Bottom L-R: Waverley Council, Waverley Council.
15: Inset: Debra Law. Waverley Council.
16: Graham Prentice
18: Bondi Rescue, Channel 9
21: Bondi Rescue, Channel 9
22: Jabiru
24-25: All images Let's Go Surfing Bondi
26: David Hahn, courtesy of Australia's Women's Weekly
27: Courtesy of Let's Go Surfing Bondi
30: Sinclair Sassen
33: Iva Villi
34: Kaz Sano
36: Main: Peter Short. Flower: Boards: Photooiasson. Barry Bennett Mal: Surfing NSW.
38: Valerie Loiseleux
40: Suljo
41: Suljo
42: Peter Short
44: Ben Jeaves
46: Steve Robertson
50: Jennifer Lawrence
52: Ben Jeaves
54: Eric Rivera
56: Jarvis Gray
58: Kaz Sano

60: Steve Robertson
64: Surf Life Saving Australia
66: Surf Life Saving Australia
68: Dmitry Maslov
69: L: Rafael Ramirez Lee. R: Waverley Council.
70: Surf Life Saving Australia
72: Courtesy of Pam Burridge
76: Kaz Sano
78: Leigh Warner
80: Richard Davies
82: Weather Map: Australian Bureau of Meteorology 2008
83: WAM Chart: Australian Bureau of Meteorology 2008
84: Steve Robertson/ASP Australasia
86: Steve Robertson/ASP Australasia
89: Kato Inowe
90: Andriy Rovenko
92: All images Mel Carswell
93: All images Mel Carswell
93: All images Mel Carswell
96: Sarah C Photography
98-99: Top L-R: John Casey, Sarah C, Jon Helgason, Tomas Kraus. Bottom L-R: Andreas Gradin, Skip O'Donnell, Homestudiofoto, Michael Ledray.
100: Rest
101: All images Sarah C Photography
102: Tim Starkey
103: Christopher King
104: Jrothe
105: All images Alan Lemire
106: Robert Lerich
107: Sarah C Photography
110: Andrew McIntosh,
Ocean Photography
112: Johnny Lye
113: Sarah C Photography
114: Dicid
116: Brian Finestone
117: Sarah C Photography
118: Andrew Davis
120: Main: Murray Swift. Inset: Quiksilver/Roxy
122: Dreamstime
124: Chiya Li
125: Top: Titelio. Bottom: Sarah C Photography.
126: Jimmy Lopes
127: Nalukai
128: All images Sarah C Photography
129: Top: Mike Thomas. Bottom: Sarah C Photography.
131: All images Sarah C Photography
132: Brent Reeves

134: Benton Duthie
136: Sarah C Photography
139: Courtesy of Barton Lynch
140: Victoria Purdie
143: Let's Go Surfing Bondi
144: Maria Bobrova
147: Mark Atkins
148: Andrew McIntosh, Ocean Photography
150: Jarvis Gray
152: All images Sarah C Photography
153: All images Sarah C Photography
154: Kaz Sano
156: All images Sarah C Photography
157: All images Sarah C Photography
158: Kaz Sano
160: Sarah C Photography
162: Ted Grambeau and Jason Childs,
courtesy of Rip Curl
164: Christopher Zachary
165: Andrew McIntosh, Ocean Photography
167: Top: Andrew McIntosh, Ocean Photography.
Middle: Surfing Australia. Bottom: Andrew McIntosh,
Ocean Photography.
168: Jarvis Gray
169: Andrew McIntosh, Ocean Photography
170: Andrew McIntosh, Ocean Photography
172: Sarah C Photography
174: Surfing Action Around The World Magazine
Feb 1969
176: Bruce Brown Films
178: All images Sarah C Photography
179: All images Sarah C Photography
181: All images Sarah C Photography
183: Andrew McIntosh, Ocean Photography
184: Roza
186: Kane Skennar
188: Eugene Tan
190: Eugene Tan
192: Sburel
194: Andrew McIntosh, Ocean Photography
197: Nalukai
199: Rahjahs
201: Jeff Walthall
203: Eric Rivera
204-205:Top L-R: Heather Craig, Tina Lau, Kaz Sano,
Christophe Michot, Jeff & Courtney Crow, Duncan
Oakes. Bottom L-R: Tina Lau, Heather Craig,
Les3photo8, Kaz Sano, Jennifer Lawrence, Plaquon.
206: Kaz Sano
208: Newspix/Virginia Young
211: Scott Rothstein
212: Susinder
214: Rafael Ramirez Lee

216: Simon Chipper
218: Sburel
219: Stephen Coburn
221: Catalin Pobega
222: Jo Charlton
224: Alex Bramwell
227: Top L-R: Renate Micallef, Ian Scott.
Middle L-R: Tomislav Zivkovic, Erika Antoniazzo.
Bottom L-R: Jxpfeer.
229: Sjanie Gonlag
230: Sarah C Photography
231: Surfing NSW
232: Scott Rothstein
234: Andrzej Tokarski
235: Max Blain
236: Wavereley Council
238: Phillip Lange
240: Andrew McIntosh, Ocean Photography
243: Glenn Jenkinson
224: Brad Morgan
246: Robert Paul Van Beets
248: Christopher Meder
249: Lauren Cameo
250: Johnny Lye
251: Ximagination
253: Waverley Council
259: Marc Dietrich
260: Sarah C Photography
262: Waverley Council
263: Waverley Council
264: Arthour
268: Trio Café
269: Ravesi's
272: Sarah C Photography
275: Grandma Takes A Trip
278: Surf Life Saving Australia
281: Timothy Starkey
282: Lamrock Lodge
284: Waverley Council
286: Steve Lovegrove
288: Kirsty Shadiac
289: Debra Law
290: Jabiru
292: Gprentice
294: Sarah C Photography
296: Sarah C Photography
299: Sarah C Photography
300: Julia Britui
302: MBPHOTO
304: Vangelis
308: Suljo
309: Suljo
316: Fernando Soares

My surfing scribbles

LOCALITY GUIDES

The series is growing

Current titles available

WWW.LEARNTOSURFGUIDES.COM.AU